ECLIPSED

OVERCOMING DISEASE, DESPONDENCY AND DOLDRUM

AKSHATA ACHARYA

ISBN 979-8-89186-926-4

*During an eclipse, it feels like the moon is covered
with a dark circle, but does that mean that
the eclipse robs the moon of its light?*

To my people, who, no matter what, always help me elevate my game:

My parents and sister, for keeping me sane all this while! Nothing without you three!

~Everything~

Contents

Preface..9

A Sneak Peek into the World of TB 13

The Day I Started Writing This Book:
An Excerpt From My Diary 19

PART ONE: The Waning.. 21

  1. Life Before Tuberculosis 23

  2. The Diagnosis 31

  3. The *(Not-So)* Shorter Regimen......................37

  4. A New Hope! 48

  5. Why So Foul?...56

  6. Ouch My Feet!!!...69

  7. Living With Neuropathy 82

  8 Bitter Ending or Better Beginning?................90

PART TWO: The Waxing.. 99

  9. Grounding Myself 101

  10. Spotting My Greenlights 113

  11. Comfortable in My Skin...............................124

  12. Finishing Strong 129

  13. What's Next?..134

Contents

A Day Before I Submitted the Manuscript:
An Excerpt From My Diary *139*
Acknowledgment *141*
Notes/Reference *143*

Preface

Why am I really writing this book? What is it that I truly want to put across through this medium? What do I want the readers, especially the patients and their families to scoop out from my experience? Will they be scared? Will they blame me for unnecessarily spreading fear? Will they think twice before recommending my book to someone else?

These are some of the questions I had asked myself while I was contemplating whether or not I should be documenting my experience. I am fully conscious that others undergoing the same treatment might have gone through greater degrees of pain than I did. Yes, TB treatment *is* painful. With my conscience intact, I am also considering all those who are just about to start their treatment. I am caught in two minds: what if this piece reprises the anxiety that some patients have managed to tame; or worse, what if it spreads a tide of fear in those who are religiously taking medications without having any major side effects. Reading this shouldn't demoralize them or their families. However, on the other hand, I feel like putting out a word to address some of the things about the disease which I learned only after being diagnosed with it. A cavalier approach towards my treatment cost me a lot, which I wish to avoid for other people who, God forbid, have to go through it tomorrow. My goal is not to create a heavy atmosphere or reinforce the stigma associated with the disease. It's not! My hope is to create a platform that encourages greater dialogue about the disease and its different aspects so that we can work towards eradicating it at the earliest.

By keeping my story as a vantage point, I am earnestly trying to direct the readers' attention towards a bigger cause. India, as of 2023, happens to be the TB capital of the world. We are at the top when it comes to the number of infected cases as well as the mortality rate. The lengthy course of TB medicines and the injections take a serious toll on a patient's physical *and* mental health. It's more than *just* popping the tablets. DID WE KNOW THIS? I never knew about this until I had it. Reading the statistics shook me to my core. I wondered why there was such little discussion around the subject in schools and colleges. TB doesn't just affect your lungs. It can affect any of your body parts except your hair and nails. Apart from the areas that get infected, what's more, over the period of years, TB has developed a variant which resists the drugs, making the treatment even harder and brutal. Why are we not made more aware of these things? It's saddening and frustrating. Hence, I also intend to reach out to those who have no idea as to what TB *really* is.

In the subsequent chapters, while discussing how the toxicity of the drugs affected my physical and mental health, I haven't deliberately missed out on any of the details. With treatment that goes on for two or sometimes more than two years, a lot of things do change. The ramifications of the disease are reflected in other, sometimes absolutely unexpected, areas of our lives. Through the book, I also try to go beyond the disease and talk about the greater damage—personal and professional—that, in some ways, is irreparable. Having said that, I also feel I have embraced some of my solid learnings during these years. So, in a way, TB was a blessing in disguise, for it lent me an entirely new way of looking at myself. Therefore, this book is a conscious effort to connect with all the patients and survivors and emphasize that, yes, you are not alone. I don't mean to inspire people. I fully understand that I am not that big of a person to do so; instead, I intend to empower them with my words. Even if there is one person who, after reading this, decides to give their treatment and their life one more chance, I will be more than happy to have brought them back. It will at least give me satisfaction that I could change one mind.

Take your tablets, no matter how bad they taste. They are going to help you lead a better life. I know it's hard. Been there, done that. A few years down the line, when you are actually living the day that you had longed for, you will pat your own back for being brave and for having swallowed thousands of those pills.

MAKE IT HAPPEN. ONE DAY AT A TIME. YOU ARE WINNING EVERY SINGLE DAY.

Let our lives after TB not just be about surviving but also thriving. Cheers!

A Sneak Peek into the World of TB

Before really delving into my story, I feel it is extremely necessary to provide a rough context and pen down a few details about the disease. Having spoken to so many people about my journey, I was moved to see the surprising reactions of the people: yes, even the most educated ones seemed blown away after learning about the different tangents of the disease and its possible, sometimes long-lasting effects on the patient. I am not exaggerating when I say that literally everyone looked dumbfounded and stumped!

Here is my small yet sincere attempt to summarize everything that I have read and learned in the past two years about this ever-ticking time bomb!

Tuberculosis is one of the oldest yet relatively misunderstood diseases throughout the world. TB is an infectious disease caused by a type of bacteria called *Mycobacterium Tuberculosis.* Every year, millions of people across the globe are diagnosed with TB, which makes it one of the top 10 deadliest diseases in the world.

TYPES OF TB:

TB is an airborne disease, meaning it can spread through air. The bacteria enter the body through the nose and may remain dormant in the body for years. This condition is called *Latent TB*. However, when there is a dip in the immunity, this infection can become active, and the patient progresses from having *Latent TB* to having *Active TB*.

SITE OF INFECTION:

Once the patient has advanced to an Active TB stage, they can experience different symptoms depending upon the site of infection. If the bacillus starts multiplying in the lungs, a person is said to have *Pulmonary Tuberculosis*. As the lungs are infected, such patients are likely to transmit the disease to other people through air while speaking, singing, sneezing, and coughing.

They may observe persistent coughing for more than three weeks or even hemoptysis (coughing blood). Since coughing is a more prominent symptom, many people associate TB with just coughing. But, of course, there is more to it.

If the bacteria attack any organ other than lungs—it could be the brain, spinal cord, kidneys, stomach, or intestine—absolutely anywhere other than hair and nails—then the patient is said to have *Extrapulmonary Tuberculosis (EPTB)*.

The symptoms could be observed in the form of swollen lymph nodes, unexplained weight fluctuation, loss of appetite, and night sweats (the last three symptoms are also common in Pulmonary TB).

Since the site of infection is outside the lungs, patients generally do not observe coughing. It also negates their possibility of transmitting the disease to other people.

Hence, it rules out the myth that TB is 'always' contagious.

Thus, depending on the site of infection—whether it is inside the lungs or outside the lungs—TB is categorized into Pulmonary and Extrapulmonary TB. **With this understanding, the common misconception that TB = Lungs / Coughing is also busted!**

TREATMENT:

Once the diagnosis is done, it is revealed whether a patient has drug-susceptible or drug-resistant TB. I am not diving deeper into 'how' the diagnosis is done because people from non-medical backgrounds cannot really understand such technical terms. But yes, the diagnosis is the most crucial part, as it decides the actual course of treatment.

Drug Susceptible TB is an infection wherein the bacteria react to all the available anti-TB drugs. The treatment lasts up to six to eight months.

Drug-Resistant TB (DRTB) is the type of TB in which the mutation of *Mycobacterium Tuberculosis* leaves the bacteria resistant to one or more anti-TB drugs. This, in turn, is divided into two categories: multidrug-resistant TB (MDR) and extensively drug-resistant TB (XDR). Considering the mutation, the patient is bombarded with strong doses of medicines; hence, the treatment can go up to two or sometimes more than two years.

Depending upon the drug susceptibility, the patient is given different combinations of drugs. Therefore, the treatment for DR-TB is more lengthy, toxic, and cumbersome.

TB IN INDIA:

As of 2023, India has been one of the top countries in the world to bear the total number of cases. Lakhs of people die every year due to TB. What makes the situation even more dire is the increasing population, since TB (in case of pulmonary TB) spreads through air.

CHANGES IN THE TREATMENT:

In terms of treatment, many changes have taken place over the years. Injections are getting replaced with oral tablets such as Bedaquiline and Delamanid, making the treatment as less painful as possible. Also, with the introduction of shorter regimens like BPaL, efforts are being made to reduce the duration of drug-resistant TB treatments. However, there have been a variety of opinions regarding shortening the duration of the treatment.

CONCLUSION:

Since my intention here is to communicate the very basics, I would not like to touch upon the topics that require expertise and extensive medical background. Having simple information as a backdrop would serve my purpose of bringing the readers under a common umbrella so that I can begin narrating my story without worrying about "Will they understand what I am talking about?"

But yes, I will be more than happy to collaborate with the readers who wish to escalate the dialogue around making the technical information as communication-friendly as possible.

You can reach out to me at akshatatbhelp@gmail.com. We can definitely make something work.

The Day I Started Writing This Book: An Excerpt From My Diary

9th November, 2022

At an enthusiastic age of 24, where you are high on energy wanting to channel it into a career field that you have chosen, life throws a curveball at you, and you are somehow expected to knock it out of the park. Multidrug resistant tuberculosis, a disease that I had vaguely heard of, infected me while I was busy planning my future. What, how, why, when??? Well...I just had it, and I was fine with it, until… that's a story for the next pages!

Today, exactly a year and a half later, having gone through crazy ups and downs, I am daring to go back and document my journey so far. With shivering hands and a lumpy throat, here I begin… writing about a roller coaster ride which is yet to come to an end (yes, as of the above-mentioned date, I am still on my medications). Kudos to the road that lies ahead... I will keep updating it as I beat every single day. I am so curious to find out how the book ends!

Let's begin!!

THE WANING

"If you want to make God laugh, tell him about your plans"

– Woody Allen

CHAPTER 1

Life Before Tuberculosis

"How should I start?" The question has kept haunting me for days, so finally I decided to start with that very question and get the ball rolling, and see, I actually have a few words written down here. Not bad! Well, the traditional way to approach memoir writing would be to begin with my childhood days. So, here it is, then...

Born into an upper middle-class family to a brilliant father who was working at Reliance Company (now owns a business) and a mother who was an accountant at Abhyudaya Bank (has now taken an early retirement to spend time with her girls), I happen to be their second child. Since my elder sister (*it's just a biological glitch that makes me call her my sister, because she is more like a big brother to me*) had given my parents a hard time for four and a half years with her mischief, stubbornness, and non-sharing nature, my parents thought having a second child would mellow her down. She would learn the value of sharing and caring, and *that* is how I came into the picture. The sole reason behind my existence is the rigid nature of my elder sister, thanks to her. Had she been a good girl, I would have not been here typing this out.

Residing in Navi Mumbai, we are a happy family of four. As a child, I was always a studious nerd who topped every exam. Nobody ever dared to bother me in school because they were all terrified of my sister, who had a goon-like persona. So, more or less, for a long period of time, I was a loner. I was a quiet, submissive, no-nonsense first bencher. I wanted to make friends but never pushed myself into striking a conversation. Although I was a "Scholar Naina," deep down within, I used to feel caged and stuck, wanting to be brave enough to tell my school teachers that I wanted to be part of the drama circle (*SCHOLAR NAINA* being a Bollywood reference to highlight the fact that *meri kisi se BUNNY nahi*—*I* was super introverted!!). I wanted to act. But I was VERY shy. To elucidate more on the extent of my shyness, I will share a memory from my preschool.

One day, my maternal grandfather had randomly come to my school to pick me up. As he had arrived unannounced, he got to see 'how' I ate my tiffin. He came inside the class of chaotic toddlers, who were being fussy about eating their food. In a room full of cries and mischief, he spotted his chubby granddaughter, whose cheeks at that time were spilling off her face. I was facing a wall and quietly eating my tiffin, all by myself. No friends. No teachers. I had all the possible traits of being a "Yaa, she is cute but doesn't smile" kind of a kid. I wouldn't disagree; yes, I was very reserved, and these traits continued to dominate me right through my middle school. So, without dwelling too much upon my childhood, which was mostly flat and mundane,

I would directly jump onto the day when things started to change.

I was in eighth grade. As I said before, I wanted to act, I always wanted to see what goes on the other side of the curtain. But how was I going to do it? "Akshata, to **act**, you first need to inter**act**. Have you ever even made friends yet? So shut up and study," I used to tell myself. But one day, since I was a bright child with fluency in Marathi, my mother tongue, my teachers asked me to audition for a play that the school was going to present at a children's theater festival. It was a surreal moment, as I had gotten an opportunity without having to ask for it. I was excited and nervous in equal parts. With a throbbing heart, I went for the audition. Seeing so many children, prepared and confident, I felt like this is not my place. But somehow, I pumped myself up and went on the stage, just to end up crying and shivering. I was stumped. My teachers kindly took me away from the stage, and the next moment I realized what had just happened. I felt like a loser. Coming back home, I cried and cried and decided that I would never do it again. But…passion finds its way… Things did change!

Same time, next year the auditions were up. Considering my previous year's fiasco, the teachers did not ask me to go for it. But I was fixated on making things right this time. Even though I had decided to give up, I kept coming back to the same thought. I knew that if I crack the audition and once I am in, I can pull it off. It was just a matter of going past the fear of an audition where everybody was going to judge me. So, I came home thinking that this time I would smartly choose a piece which requires crying (*okay, okay, at the tender age of 14, I thought that was a smart move. No judgments, please!).* I went on fully prepared—confident about not being confident—and knew that the same last year's episode would repeat once I stepped on the stage and face the audience. Well, not to my surprise, it happened again. I shivered and cried my heart out. But this time I turned the fear into my favor and strength. Everybody thought I was so good since I could shed real tears while performing, and that became my first step towards embracing this make-believe business. Yes, I was in!

The interplay of dark and light in the auditorium was breaking all the shackles and freeing my spirit. The feeling of owning a platform and being a storyteller was liberating. Things were changing, and I started liking this new me. School, followed by the wonderful years at Ramnarain Ruia College, Matunga, I was living my dream life. With every new play, I was shedding my old skin. I was fortunate enough to have encountered some of the beautiful lives that touched my soul in many ways. In the company of actors, directors, writers, musicians, and different creative artists, I was blooming. I strongly knew that acting is what makes me feel alive, and hence, that is what I would like to pursue as my profession. However, my parents wanted me to complete my masters first and then take up a full-time acting job, to which I agreed. I was fine with doing just the plays and not facing the camera till I got my masters done. As the years went by, with productions after productions (and a few awards being added to my credentials), I felt confident. I knew it was finally time to start 'my struggle'. I was close to completing my masters. Auditions, self-tapes, photoshoots, rejections, and callbacks... I was ready to dive in deep. But it was January 2020, the year that pretty much changed everything in everyone's life.

2020, for me, had started on a vibrant note. I had bagged a role in an indie film which was supposed to go on the floor by February. Cracking the very first audition boosted my confidence. I felt,yes, I can do this! I was thrilled to embark upon a new journey. Intensive preparation, followed by a rigorous shoot schedule, my days were lined up. Soon I left for the shoot, which was going to happen in the interiors of Bhuj, a city in Gujarat. This was a place with no network and no internet. So, all of the crew members were unaware as to what havoc, the soon-to-be pandemic, COVID was causing all over the world. Roughly a month later, the first schedule got over, and we all took a train back to Mumbai. It was after stepping in Mumbai, that we all realized the gravity of the situation, and to our good fortune, a week after our arrival, the lockdown was announced...boooom! The energy with which I was back from my first filming experience was silenced all of a sudden. But I was fine; I kept myself busy with my college thesis, read as many books as possible, and caught up on watching foreign films. On the domestic front, everything was good. Luckily, all four of us were together, so we were having the best time of our lives. With yoga and meditation, we chose to calm the outer chaos.

We as a family were doing everything together—cooking, cleaning, cribbing, but also celebrating. Having spent a month like it was a long party, one day my mom felt a little irritation in her breast. We got her checked, and the doctors advised her to go for surgery—the lumpectomy—and remove a tiny cyst, after which she was going to be fine. I was a little upset because the day chosen by the doctor was May 5th, which happens to be my birthday. She was home in a few hours and managed to light my face up along with the candles. But this time, the party couldn't go on for long. The removed cyst turned out to be malignant, and my mother was diagnosed with breast cancer….**booom**…again…and this time it was bigger and scarier.

Although it was the first stage, the word CANCER was enough to shatter our foundation. We had recently lost my maternal aunt, who had fought a long battle with last-stage cancer for several years; it killed her one day at a time. She used to stay in the same building we did, but on a different floor, so we all had seen her suffer EVERYDAY. We were horrified to have closely witnessed the viciousness of the disease, and this time it had wickedly knocked on our door. I silently shed a few tears, so did my sister and so did my father, who was strong on the outside but was melting from within. My mother, who was very chill—at least she was good at pretending that she was—called all of us and made us sit in front of her. "Cry as much as you want today. But let it all go. Tomorrow onwards, it is going to be a new beginning where I am going to welcome positive vibes only. There isn't going to be room for negativity henceforth. So just cry and finish it off." I was baffled to hear her say those words with such powerful conviction. Something hit us all on the inside, and we decided that it's just going to be the four of us; no outside person would be allowed to meet her; firstly, due to the risk COVID had posed, and secondly, we wanted to keep her away from all those people who inadvertently bring an air of worry and concern. We just wanted to keep her happy and light while she would gloriously face her upcoming surgeries and chemotherapies. And believe me, she did.

I will just share an incident which I remember very vividly. We all knew that once she starts her chemo, the hair will come off. Few days after her first chemo, she was out of the shower. Since she just had another massive surgery—the mastectomy—she needed my help to wipe her hair. I did help her, just to realize that she had started losing her hair in bunches. I quickly tried to clean it up without her noticing it. But it was a futile attempt, and yet again, with a casual smile, she said, "I know I am losing them, but rather than losing them in bunches, one day at a time, let them all go at once. Let's get my head shaved." We agreed. The day we shaved her head, I was very restless. I was not ready to step outside my room and see her like that. But eventually I did, and I was amazed to see her pose in front of a mirror and move her hand all over her bald head, just like a baby. I silently smiled through my tears. I felt guilty for feeling the way I did, and I realized that my mom was *actually* functioning on high levels of optimism. The very next day, we got her new specs that would make her look dashing. I am not exaggerating, but she looked like a boss lady, which she was right from the beginning, but this time her bald look positively reinforced her bold personality.

With a flair for unconditional positivity, she faced every other complication that had hit her. Time was ticking, in a good way. She was fighting every single day like a tigress! Her treatment lasted for six months, and that time span was physically and mentally daunting for all of us, especially her. We managed to stay strong by each other's sides till she was successfully out of it. 17th December, 2020—she came home after her last chemo session, and that was a feeling I can't explain in words. My sister and I welcomed her home with a huge smile and a plate of pudding that we had prepared from scratch. We had our own sweet little escape party.

Now that mom was out of danger, all of us were dying to meet our friends, family members, and all our near and dear ones in person. Apart from going to the hospital, we hadn't stepped anywhere else for six months. I just wanted to hug the hell out of everybody, and that was a big revelation to me, considering that I was a socially awkward animal. On the night of 31st December, I had a blast with my then-closest friends. I was more than eager to crush 2020 under my feet and embrace the new year with wide, open arms. But little did I know as to what lay ahead. Though 2020 was officially the worst year all over the globe, 2021 came disguised as a big, happy surprise package. I had no clue what gifts it bore for me! I guess I wasn't ready for the next big boom!

#LifeIsUnpredictable

CHAPTER 2

The Diagnosis

Uptil Dec, 2020   May, 2021

Jan, 2021

I was filled with optimism, love, and enthusiasm as I saw the first light of 2021. I woke up to a dream-like morning. I felt like I could take on the world, and why not? I had *everyone* who loved me by my side, and I knew that *everything* was going to be great this year. The extended period of grief, restlessness, and worry was coming to an end. Was it? Or was it just a beautiful dream that was soon going to become a nightmare? God knows!

Right after welcoming 2021, the four of us went on a short trip to seek blessings from our holy Goddess for letting us successfully pass through a rough phase. After coming back, I knew I had to start auditioning. Although the industry hadn't gone back to being fully operative, I still had to try my luck. I didn't know how and from where to begin. The COVID restrictions had been partially lifted, but they were still there, posing certain obstacles to all those who were starting out again. The shoots were taking place out of Maharashtra, a state in India, as the fraternity was trying to anchor its foundation within the new normal. I was determined to find my way through this. Amidst the unsettling confusion about how to drive my career forward, on my domestic front, we were planning to reunite with our friends and family. We chose our father's birthday, 9th January, as an occasion to have an intimate get-together and buried ourselves in the prep. We locked the food menu, and the night before his birthday, we had a final revision of the cake recipe that my sister and I were going to bake for him.

The next morning, as I woke up to gear myself up for an exciting day, the news about a dear one's demise crashed upon me. She was my then-partner's mother. I immediately rushed out of my house. The unfathomable loss was hard to process. I had just met her on the night of the 31st. "This year was supposed to be great, then why are we hearing this shattering news on just the 9th day of 2021? Is it a sign that 2021 could possibly be worse than 2020?" I helplessly asked myself with no expectation of getting an answer. Although she wasn't directly related to me, I had dearly known her for five years. Her loss highlighted the precariousness and uncertainty which hovers upon everything which has life instilled in it. ANYTHING CAN HAPPEN! I still managed to show up for my father's birthday with mellowed-down excitement. It was ironic how I was celebrating a life while mourning a loss, but that's a bitter pill we all swallow at some point of time in our lives. 9th January is etched in my heart forever, for two completely opposite reasons!

A few days later, my friends from my theater group decided to perform a play for a digital platform. I felt an air of comfort around the plan, and it helped me calm my anxious nerves. It was a genuine effort by all of us to find a ground amid the uncertainty surrounding our work. I hopped in. We picked a date for our performance and began with the rehearsals. It was different because none of us had ever shot a play for a digital medium. The very meaning of theater was to perform in front of a live audience, but the pandemic taught us to navigate and adapt to the new ways of creating content. The day finally arrived; we shot our play and were happy to have delivered a powerful piece. It was a small achievement that helped me shed my anxiety towards making big plans. I felt normal. But I was so engrossed in doing this work that I didn't pay any heed to the increasing trend of COVID patients all over the globe. I learned that a second wave was about to crash upon the world. There was a high possibility of countries announcing lockdowns again. By March 2021, India too announced a second lockdown, and everything that was probably gaining momentum came to a standstill. The same cycle was repeating. We were at home yet again, wondering when this was all going to end.

I kept calm and started thinking about taking advantage of the situation. Since industry was working in parts and it was going to take a while for every business to go back to normal, I thought pursuing my masters in performing arts would be a great idea. I could invest my time in gaining technical training until the pandemic settles. I spoke to my parents, and they were supportive of my plans. I started mind-mapping and came up with a list of universities I could target. Since my mom had just recovered, flying abroad was not on my immediate radar, so I decided to focus on targeting FTII, Pune. The pandemic had disrupted the functioning of almost all the institutions across the world, so even FTII wasn't planning to have a new batch anytime soon. But I was keeping an eye on the news every single day.

In the middle of this mess and conundrum, one day I woke up, sometime in May, realizing that I had a swelling below my right ear. I disregarded it for a while, assuming it could be a small twist because of the bizarre positions that I sleep in. Yes, *my sleeping postures are very unhealthy*. Since it did not subside, my mother insisted on massaging the area with oils and ointments. Nothing. Then we went to our general physician, who said that the lymph node could be swollen because of a viral infection. I took the medicines he had prescribed. Still nothing. Three weeks later, since my mother had an appointment with her surgeon to have his advice on getting a precautionary hysterectomy - removal of uterus and ovaries, I insisted that I would like to consult him for my swollen lymph nodes. The surgeon advised me to go for FNAC - (Fine Needle Aspiration Cytology) before doing any biopsy. I had heard all these terms last year while my mother was going through her cancer phase. Although my heart sank a little, I knew it can't be anything major. Next day I got my FNAC done. It was a *fine* needle test, wherein I wasn't *fine* with having a needle pierced in my neck. I clenched my fists and let the doctor prick a needle into the swelling. Damn, it was painful! The lady doctor who had done my FNAC suspected that it could be TB and informed us that she would be running an extra test called GeneXpert on my sample, to which we agreed.

A few hours later, we got the reports. The FNAC concluded that I had TB and the GeneXpert results stated that I had multi-drug-resistant TB (MDR-TB) with resistance to Rifampicin, one of the important anti-TB drugs. Also, in one of the columns, it was visible that my infection levels were exceptionally high. I wasn't shocked. I was totally fine because *I was feeling fine.* I did not have a cough; I wasn't spitting blood. Nor was I experiencing anything abnormal apart from the swelling. I always associated TB with coughing, so I did not understand what form of TB was this and what was MDR? I didn't understand a word. The reports seemed scary to read, but I could not associate them with *my* reports. It didn't make sense as to what exactly was scary about just a 2cm swelling!

We went to the same surgeon with my reports. He explained that MDR-TB is a different form of TB and that it can affect any body part, and not just the lungs, which was a common belief or rather a misconception. He said that MDR-TB is like a variant, which, over the period of years, has become strong enough to resist the medicines used to treat TB. Hence, he said, I would be given entirely different medicines, which are distributed only by the government hospitals. No private medicals are authorized to give these medicines to the patients. He asked us to visit the nearest, fully equipped government hospital and get my medicines from there. Even after hearing this, my grounds weren't shattered. I did not anticipate the seriousness of the situation. I thought I would go to the hospital, show them my reports, and get my medicines. As simple as that. Had anyone told me at that time that a 2cm cyst was going to change the trajectory of my life, I would have laughed, thought that the person was cynical, and moved on. But stepping inside the government hospital was a cosmic start to something big that was inching towards my way, not just in terms of a disease or treatment but my life in general. A whole new chapter was ready to unfold!!

#SurpriseSurprise

CHAPTER 3

The *(Not-So)* Shorter Regimen

Uptil Dec, 2020   May, 2021

Jan, 2021   July, 2021

The government hospital was just a few miles away from my place. It was huge. I had seen it so many times on my way to college or work; it is a very famous bus stop for the local buses, but I never really thought I would have to *visit* it someday. My father and I went to the hospital and looked for the DOTS center. We spotted the lady who was distributing the medicines and stood in a queue. As my turn came in, I casually showed the lady my file and innocently asked her to give me the medicines. She looked at me, scanned me from head to toe, probably even judged me for my ignorance, and said that this is not how a patient gets their medicines. She asked my father and I to register my case in the hospital, get a case paper, and *then* meet the doctors from the department. I felt stupid because I never thought starting a TB treatment would require any process as such. Even the ads which I had seen on TV projected that a patient has to go to the DOTS center and get the pills—just like a polio center where you go and get your *"Do Boond Zindagi Ke Naam"*. I used to think every patient is given the same kind of standard treatment. I didn't know that a whole set of doctors decide which medicines to prescribe to every patient. "Is this really a big deal, or is the government hospital staff just making it seem big?" I thought. Shrugging my doubts, I went downstairs, did all the tiring paperwork, and went back to the department after an hour or so. After a few minutes, I went inside to see the doctors. The lady doctor took my file, saw every report carefully, and then took a paper to write something. She kept on writing. I was curiously looking at her. After writing two pages front and back, she handed over the papers to me and said, "These are the tests that you need to do right now. We need to have all of these reports as a baseline before deciding the right drugs and doses, after which we will hospitalize you right away. We need to observe you for a week."

WHAT??

I heard the doctor say those words like it was routine.

She offhandedly dismissed us and asked the next patient to come in. I came outside and sat on the bench. My head was spinning. I told my father that maybe this is some kind of a scam. "I am feeling normal," I said, "Then why are they creating a panic as if this is something huge? We will go back to our family doctor *(the same surgeon who had done all of my mother's surgeries during her cancer treatment and guided me with the TB diagnosis),* whom we trust, and ask him if this is standard protocol and if it is really necessary to get hospitalized." We left the hospital to see him. He said that this is how the government hospitals function, and I would have to abide by their policies. He said he will do something about the hospitalization and made a few calls to try and prevent it.

So basically, the government of India has taken an initiative to eliminate TB entirely from the country. The supply of medicines is in the hands of the government alone, and hence, a patient cannot get these medicines in any medical shop. Also, apart from the medicines, for which the patients are not charged a penny, they are also entitled to a free consultation. All of this is restricted to government hospitals only. Now, having this as a backdrop, I was assuming that the tests and hospitalization would mean nothing more than just paperwork.

I went back to the government hospital and helplessly gazed at the papers. It demanded me to have all the possible tests, right from HIV to pregnancy. The doctors did not miss out on any of the alphabets from A-Z while writing down the different names of the blood tests. I was also asked to get the fitness certificates from a psychiatrist, ENT, and ophthalmologist, and not to forget different kinds of CT scans, X-rays, and sonographies. I felt exhausted merely after reading those papers. All of these tests were time-consuming, which meant that my medicines would not start for another couple of days.

We had requested the doctors not hospitalize me. They tried explaining to me that a patient has to get his ECG done daily for a week after starting the treatment. One of the drugs can possibly affect a patient's heart rate, which is why an ECG is important. I knew that once I get hospitalized, the situation back home will be very difficult. My mother was still recovering from her surgeries, and we had planned an additional surgery, a hysterectomy, for her, just as a precaution. Our whole calculation was going to get disturbed. Since there was no need for an IV, I kept resisting. Finally, the doctors gave in to my stubbornness and waived the hospital admission. But they warned me that I would have to come for my ECG daily without fail. I said yes and went ahead with doing my tests.

Getting those tests done was like getting a tour of the hospital. I went to almost every floor and every department, every time with a different family member, for the next coming days. My mother was deliberately kept away from this hassle due to the second wave of COVID. We took maximum care and went to the hospital every single day. Finally, after a week, on 9th June, 2021, with a pile of files in our hands, my father and I went to see the doctor. He skimmed through the reports and gave a green signal to start the shorter regimen, the treatment that goes on for nine to eleven months. He took my case paper and started writing down the number of drugs. One, two, three, four, five, six, seven, and eight. "Okay, eight tablets a day won't be too much, I guess. I can manage," I said to myself. I listened to all the instructions that the doctor gave me and walked towards the DOTS center to get the medicines.

Okay, now I understand why the lady in the center had given me a stern look on my first day, when I had directly asked her for the medicines.

Lesson learned ✓

This time, with proper documentation, I asked the lady to give me the medicines. I was waiting as she took out a number of boxes from a shelf. She then started grouping them into different bundles. Once she was done, she started explaining to me, "These are the eight drugs that the doctors have prescribed you. But since the power of each drug is very high, you have to split the medicines and then take them."

To make this easier to understand, I will share an example. One of the drugs prescribed to me was named pyrazinamide. The power was 1750 mg/day. Since there is no single tablet of that higher power, I had to take three tablets: 500+500+750 = 1750 mg per day. Likewise, since the power of all the drugs was high, I realized that I had to take 19 tablets, which added up to roughly 6,000 mg per day. THAT was the first moment I got scared.

I went back to the department to ask the doctors if taking such a high dose would interrupt my work, because just a few days before I had said yes to a new play and had received a call back from another audition. I didn't want the treatment to interfere with my work in any way. The doctors assured that patients can carry their medicines wherever they go; just make sure that the timing of tablets is not missed. I was relieved. I came home with a bag full of medicines, had my lunch, and prepared myself to kick-start the treatment. My mom was very worried (So was I), because she knew how reckless I was when it came to finishing the course of antibiotics. But I promised my loved ones that I would be disciplined. My sister, who is compulsive about having things organized, prepared a chart for me and asked me to tick after taking each tablet. I took my first tablet, after 15 minutes, the second, and so on. I felt like resting but had to finish the remaining 17 ones, so I just sat and closed my eyes. After an hour, everything in my stomach started churning; I felt like throwing up. I tried not to. But looking at the next huge tablet triggered the feeling, and I threw up. My head felt heavy. I wiped my mouth and took that pill. It turned powdery as soon as I kept it on my tongue. There is no surprise as to how it tasted. I drank lots of water to get rid of all the remains. I felt another retch coming. I diverted my thoughts, considering that it could be just psychological. But I guess it wasn't. I kept throwing up after regular intervals. My father rushed me to the hospital after three hours because I was extremely dehydrated. The doctor explained that since I have MDR, the medicines would have toxic side effects and that it is like a chemo for TB. While suppressing this infection, some other areas could get affected. I felt weak. Food made me nauseous, but I had to eat. That was Wednesday. I knew that it takes 21 days for your body to adjust to anything new. I kept counting.

Eight days passed, but I kept getting worse. Because of the high-power, I had to pop in 19 tablets throughout the day—each tablet after a gap of 45 minutes. I used to wake up in the middle of the night to throw out all the acids, which kept burning my stomach. I had sleepless nights. I literally used to watch every hour of the night pass till it was morning. I was given additional medicines for acidity, nausea, and other protein supplements. I remember, very vividly, that for the first eight days I was not able to poop. My parents did everything to cure it, but the dose was so strong that it had ruined my system. My chest felt heavy, and I was not able to lie down. I told my doctors about it, but their only solution to all my complaints was MORE MEDICINES. Finally, after days of trial-and-error, I was able to empty my stomach (I had gulped down half the bottle of a laxative; I **would not recommend anyone to do it)**. I still had to go to the hospital daily to get my ECG. I then realized that getting hospitalized was not just a formality. It was necessary. I got to know about the side effects as I started experiencing them one by one. Everyone just kept pressing about getting hospitalized. No one actually spoke about the toxicity of the drugs. Had I been told the actual reason behind hospital admissions before, I would not have been adamant. Still, I was wrong not to have asked.

Lesson learned, yet again. ✓

Everyday felt like a year. Gulping down 20–22 tablets a day was not a joke. Eventually, I had to back out from the play and not attend that callback. I felt bad, but honestly, that became the least of my concerns. At that point, getting good sleep and being able to sit peacefully, doing nothing were the only ambitions I had.

I was feeling different. There was a rush in my body during the morning, which made me jump and run across my living room. Sounds weird? I will try and explain this as close to reality as possible by giving similar examples. It felt as if somebody had tied my hands and legs and had thrown me into water, asking me to swim my way through. To overcome that feeling, I felt like I had to physically fight it by walking or jumping rigorously. I was feeling claustrophobic. I just knew I had to get it all out, but due to lack of sleep, I used to feel exhausted. It bothered me while it lasted. Every day, the time between 9 a.m. to 1 p.m. was daunting. I used to continuously brisk walk in my entire house. My attempt to try and get some sleep in those hours used to backfire. Sitting in one place and closing my eyes scared me to death. I used to choke. I remember my father and my sister had gotten new board games and a new deck of cards to divert my attention from that mind boggling feeling. But every time I sat with them to play, I struggled to breathe and ultimately went back to walking or jumping. Even I used to think that was crazy - but it was what it was!! The side effects of the medicines kept compounding. My periods were extremely abnormal, I started losing my hair, I kept throwing up four times a day and had rashes all over my body. I also started experiencing joint pain. As the days were passing by, the pain elevated to such an extent that I was barely able to lift my finger. Every possible bone in my body was screaming in pain. My parents were helping me do EVERYTHING. I needed help in doing even the basic tasks like walking or sitting down. I remember being in the washroom and not being able to get up after a bath. I took support of the taps and buckets...but I kept falling. I never felt so helpless. I had almost forgotten how to walk by myself. 21 days had already passed, but rather than getting used to the treatment, my body kept resisting.

In addition to this, as if this wasn't enough, I tested positive for COVID. More medicines? Please, NOO!! My mother was positive too. That left us both in isolation for the next 14 days. Being in a confined space was a nightmare. During the morning time, as I said before, the rush in my body forced me to jump and run. But now, in a closed space and with weaker joints, I felt suffocated and miserable. It was difficult to breathe. I did not know which infection was bumming me out—TB or COVID? But to be honest, the side effects of TB were so much that COVID symptoms felt less jarring. I had terrible mood swings. My mother, who is a tigress, as I always say, brainwashed me every now and then. I kept crying. After a few days, my eyesight was weakened too. I could not tell time or read any messages on my mobile screen. Everything was blurry. I begged my mother to get me out of the pain. Nine months was going to be a long time, considering the fact that every minute was torture. I felt like a baby. I was acting like one, clinging to my mother every time I felt low. She had to see me like this—a living lump who was shedding weight one day at a time.

Since I was losing touch with reading or watching anything, not just because of the eyesight, but also because I had lost the motivation altogether, my mother was asking my close friends to cheer me up on a video call. They did. I was sane enough to know that drugs were making me feel despondent. I was trying hard to beat it and come out stronger, but I failed, and I hated it. I felt a bigger shadow behind me, but it was hard to defeat it. Is this what depression looks like? I don't know! But whatever you name it, that deep, dark space seemed very scary and trapping.

However, even in those lifeless days, I meditated and chanted. I forced myself to do that. I knew that it could be the only way to calm myself down. I was trying to make peace with those tablets, although they were adamant on being my enemies.

The feeling of being physically and emotionally dependent on my mother, who herself had just come out of a deadly disease, was killing me from within. I wanted to end it. I recalled an incident with the psychiatrist whom I had visited before starting the treatment to get my fitness certificate. She had asked me questions like, "Do you feel like hitting a random person on the road? Do you like your life? Do you feel like ending it?" I had made fun of all those questions that day. I was like, Yes, I love my life. Yes, I am ambitious; why would I want to ever end it? She also tried to make me aware by saying that the treatment could lead to severe mood swings; however, I had dismissed all those possibilities by thinking, 'I am strong and I can handle it'.

Cavalier approach: not good! Lesson learned ✓

But later, I realized why she had asked me all those questions. Yes, the medicines take a toll on your mental and physical health. They mess up your life in a big way. Honestly, although I felt like putting an end to it, I constantly kept telling myself that better days were coming. I kept shutting those horrible thoughts, knowing that the drugs were speaking that language, not me. It was hard, but I knew I had to go one minute at a time.

On the 14th day of our quarantine, after having digested more than 600 tablets, my mother said she would accompany me to the hospital. The only reason she hadn't come to the hospital yet was the risk of COVID. Now that she had had it, she wanted to meet my doctors. So in the morning, after my ritualistic throw up post-breakfast, my parents walked me downstairs and took me to the hospital. Seeing me like this, the doctors were horrified too. I was weak, almost immobile, and covered in boils. Just a month ago, I had spoken to them like an adult, and now I was being walked like a kid. They asked us to sit. Seeing the deterioration of my health, the doctors decided to put me on a longer regimen, the treatment, which lasts for 18–24 months. After hearing him say so, I had mentally stormed out of his cabin. I was reluctant to extend the treatment for two long years. I wanted to finish it off as soon as possible. I didn't want to have an extended period of pain and isolation. But they were kind enough to make me look at the brighter side, that is having different drugs and getting fewer tablets in a day. Although I had mastered the technique of vomiting (drank a glass of water just before throwing up and pulled my stomach in by giving it a slight jerk—that helped me control the burning sensation of the acids and reduce the pressure on my chest), I was tired of doing it four times a day. I wanted a change. I wanted peace. I wanted a normal life. Being reluctant and casual had already cost me a lot. So, without wasting another minute, I gave in to their words, took a leap of faith, and decided to switch from a *'not-so-shorter'* shorter regimen to a *'hope-so-better'* longer regimen.

#HighlyOptimistic

CHAPTER 4

A New Hope!

After agreeing to switch to the longer regimen, the doctors asked me to stop all my previous medications right away. I felt better because, otherwise, I had to take pills after every 45 minutes throughout the day. I was taking my first tablet at seven in the morning to make sure I swallowed all 20–22 of them before my bedtime. This had been my routine for over a month. But that day, even though it was 11.50 a.m. and I was due for my next tablet, I was asked not to take it. That was my first 'aha moment' in a long time. We were supposed to surrender all the older medicines to the DOTS center and get the new ones. I was relieved to know that in the longer regimen, I would have to take only nine tablets every day. The dose was decided by keeping my weight in mind. **"Huh? Just nine?"** I asked casually. After gulping down 600 of them, nine in a day felt petty. It was nothing. Although the increasing joint pain was a concern (as the toxicity of previous medicines had wrecked my bones), the doctors assured me that it would subside in a few months. The new drugs were going to be less harmful and more tolerable. My parents felt reassured. Our visit to the hospital was time-consuming; I had not had a tablet for over two hours. SUCH A RELIEF! I was somewhat happy thinking that today onwards, I will not have to sit by the clock and watch every hour pass. Still, I wanted to be 100% sure, so even though my parents were helping me walk towards our car, I was busy using my fragile fingers to recount and reconfirm the number of tablets I would have to take.

Bedaquiline: 100 mg + 100 mg = Two tablets [Thrice a week].
Levofloxacin: 500 mg + 250 mg = Two tablets
Clofazimine: 100 mg = One tablet
Cycloserine: 250 mg + 250 mg = Two tablets
Linezolid: 600 mg = One tablet
Pyridoxine: 100 mg = One tablet

Maximum of nine tablets in a day, confirmed ✓

We were home by 1–1.30 p.m. My parents settled me into my room and walked outside just to hear me say, "I am hungry. Can we have lunch?" My parents, to their utter surprise, stopped and turned around, saying, "What? What? What?" (just kidding). In my head, I gave that moment a dramatic flair because I was feeling hungry after almost a month. Without wasting a minute, my dad rushed into the kitchen and got me a plate of hot *chapati and sabzi.* It was cauliflower curry, I remember. I was greedily eating everything off the plate. My parents literally saw me eat that *chapati* with pride as I was smacking my lips and asking for one more. Me getting back my appetite within the first few hours was the first positive sign. Yes, the physical pain was still there, but, on the inside, I was feeling like a baby—excited about doing even the smallest of things. I WAS GOING TO REST FOR A WHILE! I WAS FEELING LIKE TAKING A NAP!! YES!

After taking a cozy nap on a rainy afternoon, I took my new medicines and crossed my heart. Two hours had passed, and everything was normal. I wasn't feeling nauseous. My head felt a little heavy, but that wasn't much of a problem. I sighed with relief. In the evening, just to cheer me up, my uncle and aunt decided to celebrate his (my uncle's) birthday with us at our place. Maybe I wasn't able to clap that well, but I surely sang out loud. That night still remains the most peaceful night of my life ever. We tend to take basic things, like getting a good night's sleep, for granted. Yes, there was some discomfort because of the body ache, but that night, I sure as hell slept like a baby!

Here, I would like to digress a little and say something about my initial Shorter Regimen TB treatment. The treatment was extremely brutal and painful. The high-power drugs did not suit me at all. I wasted a month taking intense medication that messed up with my life in a big way. Although that period lasted for 'just a month', every passing second was a nightmare. Till date, I keep asking myself a question: What if I would have agreed to get hospitalized? Had I not resisted, the doctors could have monitored my health better and could have changed my line of treatment within the first few days itself. I was wrong about not getting hospitalized, but I don't regret it. I resolutely denied it because, at that point, I was trying to put my mother first.

I can never go back and make-up for that one month I have wasted and suffered, but I can definitely ask other patients to 'carefully comply' with the hospital policies and not create unnecessary agony for themselves. Also, during those days, I kept thinking that my body would eventually cope with the medicines. I strongly knew that I wasn't feeling fine. My appetite was lost, my bones were wrecked, I was throwing up four times a day, my body was covered with boils and rashes, and I eventually had become a living baggage. I used to tell myself that cancer patients also throw up during their chemo days. So maybe it is normal for these medicines to have such racking side effects. I had reluctantly made peace with the fact that this is how my life will be for the next nine months. Later, I overheard my mother tell some of our family members that even she did not have such serious side effects from her chemotherapy sessions. She felt bad, but she kept elevating my spirit, encouraging me to not give up. Today, she might be feeling bitter about 'encouraging' me or for 'pushing' me through those days because none of us were aware as to what range of tolerance a patient should have while taking the medicines. What I was going through was well outside the normal range.

I am earnestly requesting the patients to immediately report any abnormalities that they observe to their doctors. **Going through the pain that makes you uncomfortable from within is not a sign of normalcy.** Except for the first few days of your treatment, wherein it is common to feel a little nauseous and dizzy, you should eventually eat better, and sleep better. I am saying this because the drugs have improved in the past few years. Efforts are being made to replace the injectable drugs with more effective oral tablets. Please listen to your body, your doctors, and take the medical staff into confidence as and when required.

Now, coming back to my story, the days that followed later were pretty breezy. My parents were helping me roll over to the other side of the bed or stretch my legs on the couch. I was still chirpy because what I thought would go on for nine months or even a year had dramatically come to an end after a month. All my friends were coming over to meet me in person. Although the new treatment was going to be longer, I was fine, as it did not seem to have many side effects. I was 100 percent sure that these tablets would not create much of a problem. "Once I am able to walk properly, I can resume my work," I thought. Till the time I am bedridden-ish, I will try to be as happy as possible. I resumed my voracious reading, now that my vision was clear. To reinforce the gratitude, I also watched all the feel-good movies and celebrated the fact that I was comforting myself in physical discomfort.

A month had passed. The happy puppy phase was fading. Eventually I got bored of just sitting all day long, not having much to do. Don't get me wrong, I was still brimming with gratitude, but I wanted to engage myself into doing some more productive work. The joint pain hadn't gone yet, so even though I was ready to take up work, the physical restrictions kept me on the backfoot. Acting was clearly out of question. I was wondering what else I could do.

I had heard my family members tell me that I am good with words. I used to write blogs during my college years about random slice-of-life stories. After reading them, I was encouraged by them to write more, but I somehow ignored it, thinking that they are creating hype. Family is a place where you are loved no matter what; your creativity is praised, so I never took their advice *that* seriously. But being bedridden compelled me to go back and rethink upon their suggestion. I was planning to give it a shot. But how? I wanted to write but didn't know how to use it in a professional realm. I also did not want a conventional '9–5' corporate job. I wanted something where I could learn while having fun with it. That's when Ameya Mondkar, then an acquaintance and now a dear friend, came to my rescue. Ameya had recently given birth to his start-up kid, an insanely unconventional branding agency by the name of Fiction Foxx. I knew him from my theater days through mutual friends. Considering his work vibe, which is a wonderful amalgamation of madness, creativity, and professionalism, I asked him if he could suggest a workplace that could fit me in. He knew about my treatment and had also read a few of my writing samples. Hence, he suggested that I should consider joining the copywriting department at Fiction Foxx if it interests me. He assured 100 percent time flexibility and zero percent '9-5 office' feels.

What more could I have asked for??

I immediately saw it as a green flag. I was dying to be a busy bunny again, so I hopped on like one.

I was more than eager to explore the world of copywriting. It's differently interesting than what I had assumed it would be. Ameya, being a great mentor, kept dropping his pearls of wisdom and guided me whenever I stumbled upon an obstacle. Having a firsthand experience of directly dealing with the clients, working closely with their goals, and bringing out powerful deliverables were some of the things that sort of brought me back to the real world. I was spending my days learning a new skill set.

I am intentionally taking these names because, it is through Fiction Foxx, that I was able to spot my first green light in the journey so far. I may or may not have said it directly, but today, through this medium, I am officially saying that I am filled with gratitude for the opportunity that Fiction Foxx gave me. In such uncertain times, what you need is ephemeral support from the right people who make your journey less cumbersome and more memorable.

As I was getting acquainted with the new tools of writing, I wanted to try something for myself as well. I wanted to challenge myself by writing a short fictional story. For days, I kept staring at the blank page, and to overcome the guilt, I finally started with typing out just two words: short story!

Bummer, right??

But back of my mind, I kept thinking about catching a good moment to create my fiction around, and eventually I did develop a few concepts. I wrote a few shorter-format screenplays. I am sure when the time is right, those short films will see the light of day.

So, two months had passed since the beginning of my new treatment. Slowly, the joint pain had started to subside. I was regular with my follow-ups and disciplined about taking the medicines on time. I also started going out for brief outings with my friends. Observing steady progress made me confident about taking up new acting assignments. My skin color was changing (More on this in Chapter 11), but I was fine with these side effects as long as they were just 'external'. Were they? I guess not. After two months of joy and fun, it was time for me to find out what was going on the 'inside'. The next big thing had already started inching my way. I was going to learn about it anytime soon!

Boom again? Let's find out.

#NotAgain

Why So Foul?

It was September, 2021. Two months passed since I began my new treatment. I was deeply engrossed in exploring the world of copywriting. The joint pain was getting better. Life had somewhat become normal-ish. I was all set, again, to make some new plans for myself. I was being asked if I was interested in being an assistant to a renowned critically acclaimed Hindi film director (can't take the name). I wanted to grab that opportunity, but I had to keep it on hold. I felt like I could take up that job after a month or so when I have complete control over my mobility. I was looking forward to having a new beginning ahead.

Meanwhile, we had a Ganpati celebration at my native place. I was meeting my relatives after a long time. I had a good time with all of my family members. Because of the medicines, I did have certain restrictions when it came to having food, so I was bound to have a healthy diet. But with my cousins by my side, my mom agreed for me to have one small cheat meal. We went to a famous spot to have my favorite misal with *tarri*, a spicy curry on top. I relished every bite of it. Once I was done eating, I asked my father (with a puppy face) if I could have a *vada pav*. He seemed to melt and secretly permitted me to have it, just once. Although I was strict about my diet, I badly wanted a cheat day to satisfy my taste buds. I was sincere but I needed a little deviation. I promised that this is a one-time thing and that I will not let myself loose.

After a few days, we came home. I was due for my monthly follow-up. I told my parents that now I am getting better, and so from there onwards, I can manage to go to the hospital all by myself. They agreed. I took a cab, went to the hospital, stood in a line to get a case paper, and got myself checked. Since my appetite was good and joint pain had slowly started to subside, the doctors did not ask me to get any blood tests done. I was happy because having a blood test after regular intervals had become a routine. All of us were relieved that finally the side effects of previous medicines were vanishing and that the new treatment was suiting me.

Just when I thought I was coping, THAT day arrived - 16th September, 2021. We had had our lunch late in the afternoon, so none of us were that hungry at night. Since I have always been a cooking enthusiast, loving to experiment in the kitchen, I suggested that I would prepare dal khichdi with tadka for all of us. I went into the kitchen and started chopping the veggies. I sensed that something was rotten. I assumed it could be from somewhere outside and ignored it. After putting all the spices in the oil, the foul smell intensified. I realized that this was coming from our kitchen, so I called my mother to check if the dal was rotten. She checked and said that everything was fine. Keeping my doubts aside, I managed to prepare the khichdi. With a dull face, I served our plates and gave them a heads up that something might be wrong with the dish and that I am not happy with the way it smells—re-stressing the fact that dal was rotten. I kept staring at their faces as they had their first spoonful. I expected them to pass a lame comment, but I was taken aback when they all smacked their lips, saying that it was yum!!

YUM?? REALLY??

I ate a spoonful of it and kept it aside, declaring that I cannot stand the taste. Instead, I took a glass of milk and started drinking it. The same thing happened again. As I had a first sip, I made an ugly face and immediately spat it out in the sink. The milk is rotten, I said. My mom took my glass to have a sip. She said it was totally fine. I lost my head because what was 'evidently rotten' for me was 'yum' for them. I went into my room feeling a bit overwhelmed. "What is going on? Do I have hyperacidity? What if mom finds out that I had a vada pav that day? Is it because of the spicy food? Sh*t!! Everyone is going to be mad at me." I kept blaming myself for having that cheat meal. Scared and baffled, I decided not to go outside and sleep as early as possible.

I woke up the next day, realizing that I had a bad, metallic taste in my mouth. Even the normal air felt *garbage-ish* while breathing. I went to brush my teeth. I was lost in my thoughts as I started brushing. But I bounced back immediately because even the toothpaste had a horrible taste. I thought after having a good night's sleep, this thing would go away, but it didn't. I kept mum and joined everyone for breakfast. My mom had made poha. The minute she served my plate,

I asked her to back off, saying that it smelled exactly like yesterday's dal khichdi - FOUL. I got mad, thinking I might have COVID again. So I went on smelling everything in the house—soaps, perfumes, oils, shampoos—everything had a peculiar rotten smell. I felt I was going to explode. I was unable to understand what was happening. It was just me who was experiencing this paranoia in the house. I hadn't LOST my sense of smell and taste, which was a classic COVID symptom. Instead, I had a DISTORTED sense of smell and taste. This can't be COVID, I thought, then what else could it be? A new side effect of my TB medicines?

NOOOOO!!!

I locked myself up in a room, firstly because I was not ready for a new toss, and secondly it was hard for me to tolerate even the faintest of the smells. My sister insisted that we should go to the hospital and let our doctors know. I agreed. I wrapped my face up to avoid any outside smells and went to the hospital.

"Just gargle with mouthwash; it will go away," the doctors suggested. I tried hard to explain that even the mouthwash tastes disgusting right now, but my efforts went down the drain. I came back home feeling disheartened and went for a hot shower, thinking it might help me calm down. Instead, the so-called 'fragrance' of the body wash triggered the foul smell and made me feel worse. I wasn't able to tolerate my own body odor. "I smell pathetic; please don't come near me," I kept telling my parents. I buried myself under a blanket, trying to escape. But what was I going to escape from? The foul smell *was me*. I could not get rid of it whatsoever. I kept telling my parents that I felt like I was made to sit inside a heap of garbage. Everything stunk.

Because of the new, unidentified condition, my eating patterns were disturbed. I was feeling hungry, but the food made me nauseous. For example, I used to feel like having dal-rice, but when it was brought in front of me, it smelled and tasted horrible. It was this gap—wherein I was able to recollect the original smell or taste of a dish but that did not match with what it *actually* smelled or tasted like - made me feel miserable. It was different from feeling loss of appetite or feeling nauseous. I had experienced drug-induced nausea before, and it definitely wasn't that. I was feeling hungry, but the intense smell and taste canceled out on my food options. Having tablets on an empty stomach made me throw up. I was caught up in a vicious cycle. I just wanted to know what was causing this. I prayed that it shouldn't be a side effect of the new TB medicines, or else I would have to live with it for the next two years. Finally, after cribbing for hours, I gathered myself and started looking for information on the internet. I typed out my symptoms and started hunting for a relevant source of information.

After going through various medical sites, I finally found one article which exactly described what I was going through. It had compiled the cases of all those patients from across the globe who observed this sudden change. A girl was bathing three times a day as she felt conscious of her body odor. Some other middle-aged woman had a complaint that one day, while having dinner with her partner, she felt that wine tasted like gasoline. There was another man who reported that everything tasted like garbage. All these descriptions matched what I had been feeling. By looking at the similarity, it felt as if I myself had written it. I kept reading the article, and finally, at the end of it, it was mentioned that all those patients had witnessed this distortion a few months after recovering from COVID. This was a rare post-COVID symptom called 'Parosmia'.

Post-covid parosmia was and still is a lesser-known condition. In a situation where the doctors were struggling to study covid and its medicines, expecting them to know everything about bizarre post-covid symptoms was unrealistic. Even they were getting acquainted with new conditions as and when a patient came up with a new and weird complaint. In my case, I was already on MDR drugs. So which condition is causing what was quite complex to find out.

But what is Parosmia??

So basically, a person observes parosmia two-three months after recovering from covid. To put it in simple terms, the Corona virus destroys the cells and nerves in your nose while you are infected. The neurons die, causing anosmia, the loss of smell and taste, a typical symptom which many patients had, including myself. These olfactory cells are connected to your brain. During the recovery process, it is possible that these cells connect to the wrong spots in the brain, creating a sense of distortion, resulting in a condition known as parosmia. Because of this damage, the brain is not able to detect which smell is what or which taste is what. The distortion occurs randomly, as in, a person can all of a sudden start experiencing a foul taste or a rotten smell, but it may take time for the condition to reverse. There is no specific time; the reversal may take a few weeks, several months, or even a year, varying from person to person (in my case, complete recovery did not happen as of November 2023; parosmia lasted for more than 2 years).

Although the air around me was still *unbreathable,* once I knew what condition I had, I felt less paranoid. Knowing that this is not any side effect from TB drugs, I sighed with relief. As I kept reading other material regarding parosmia, I learned about different kinds of food which possibly trigger the condition: onions, garlic, meat, milk, eggs, chocolates, and so on. Having a hot meal was another trigger for this condition; hence, having plain, cold food was recommended by the experts. I also found YouTube channels like 'AbScent' wherein the research scientists were helping other patients to cope based on their tried and tested methods. I quickly made a list of all the dos and don'ts and learned what else can be done to improve the condition.

I eventually started looking for a potential cure. Sadly, there was no cure as such for this. However, there was olfactory training and smell therapy, which helped in making the recovery process faster. Since parosmia is a result of 'the wrong wiring', the connections in the brain need to be 'rewired'. Smell therapy involves training the brain by exposing it to the same series of scents on a daily basis. What a patient has to do is take three–four scents, like essential oils or anything that has a strong and, more importantly, a familiar fragrance. After closing the eyes, a person should smell each of those scents for 15–30 seconds and recollect the original fragrance in order to bring the actual smell memory back to the brain. The cycle has to be repeated twice a day.

In my case, I picked up lavender oil, eucalyptus oil, and a lemon. I had read all the instructions carefully, so I started practicing this daily. Also, it involved using home or kitchen products; hence, it wasn't risky to do it without anybody's consultation. The therapy didn't work overnight; the lemon did not smell like a lemon, quite obviously, but I was less paranoid and more focused on getting myself healed. I had to fix my eating problem. I was trying hard to cope because not eating anything was not an option for me. I started having bland food or fruits and avoided anything that was spicy or oily. No rice, no dal, no chapati. However, this altered diet was not sufficient for me considering my TB background. I was throwing up every day. Also, I was sitting in a different room because the very air that I was inhaling felt disgusting. It was during this parosmia phase that I realized how important the sense of smell and taste are. The very aroma of the garlic tadka (just a random example), which used to make me drool, was now making me nauseous. I was a hard-core spicy eater, but all my favorite dishes were now out of my sight. Taste and smell can be *soooooo* subjective! It's crazy!

Speaking of subjectivity, this shift made me think a lot, and that's when it occurred to me: what if we all have our own unique way of smelling and tasting everything? Just think about it. Some people hate papaya, but some of them just love it. Some could savor a pork dish, but some might just feel pukish after eating it. The same could be applicable to fragrance as well. Maybe your mother could be a fan of an ayurvedic-chemical-free soap but your sister just can't stand the smell of it. You may love using a flowery perfume, but your partner feels it's 'too sweet' and hence disregards your choice. Doesn't that happen very often? We can think about the chances of each individual being instilled with a different ability to perceive a smell or a taste. Well, what if this very theory of mine could be the reason behind us saying, *Ahh, we have similar tastes!*

Possible, isn't it? Having gone through this shift, I feel it is!!

My thoughts were running haywire, but my body was weak. After a week or so, I was all wan and chalky. When my health started deteriorating even more, on 26th September, 2021, I was rushed to the hospital. I had almost seen that coming. After getting the tests done, the doctor said that my blood reports were very poor. The hemoglobin level had dropped down to 7 and WBC was way below range. I was immediately hospitalized. We thought it could be because of parosmia, but I never dared to tell my doctor that I had read about this piece on the internet. I was scared of them labeling me as "she tries to be too smart". I kept my mouth shut and got myself hospitalized. Considering my weight and overall health, the doctor decided to stop all my TB medicines for a while. He wanted to observe a gradual rise in my Hb levels. For me, everything was new. I was slurping spicy *tarri* 15 days ago and cut to—there I was lying on a hospital bed with my hands all swollen due to back-to-back needle pricking, the injections, and the saline bottles. I had never been hospitalized before. For me, it was more painful because all my veins had shrunk due to the medications, so every day the nurses had to prick at a new spot to give me the IV. Eventually, the nurses got me a baby needle to make the pricking less painful.

While I was in the hospital for eight days, everyone was getting me something to eat. It was a trial-and-error thing to see if I was getting any better at tolerating different tastes and smells. It was easy to do so when I was home, but having sent a variety of meals to the hospital just for me to dismiss all of them, it was a tedious task for those who were sending me tiffin.

As a child, I always used to think hospitalization was so cool. People get you flowers and fruits while you rest and sleep for the whole day. However, I tasted the reality, and it was gruesome. Also, this gruesome 'taste' of reality wasn't a result of 'parosmia'; hospitalization will truly be distasteful under any given circumstance.

I am digressing once again to highlight an incident in the hospital. One afternoon, when I was done with my lunch, a nurse came in to give me a bottle of saline. She started the dose and asked me to sleep, as she had kept the speed on low. A little later, I rang the bell and asked to pause it as I had to go to the loo. After coming back, she re-inserted the saline needle and left the speed on high. She must have been in a hurry, and I was even feeling sleepy, so I ignored it. The saline bottle, which was supposed to get over in three hours, was emptied in an hour. Some other nurse came in and took out the needle.

After a while, I started shivering. My father tried putting two-three extra blankets, but I kept getting the chills. We realized that the speed was relatively higher than what it was supposed to be; hence, I was feeling shivery. It was so cold that my teeth were chattering. I don't know why, but I started crying. - it wasn't anything serious, nor was anyone at fault, but after seeing me cry, one of the housekeeping ladies came in to check on me. She was skinny, 40-something. After looking at my waterworks, she was a little welled up too. She came near me to ease me out. I guess she was aware of my TB treatment. "My husband," she said, "is a leprosy patient. He can't do anything on his own, but he isn't ready to give up. He still insists on not getting any help and managing his routine on his own. Apart from working in this hospital, I am also an ASHA worker (ACCREDITED SOCIAL HEALTH ACTIVIST, who are female healthcare activists trained to facilitate the work of the nationwide public health system within their community). Instead of taking care of him, my husband wants me to take care of the TB patients. I leave my husband alone to make sure that TB patients are getting proper care. Now tell me, my child, if you cry, how will that make a worker like me feel? You have parents and good medical support to ensure your speedy recovery. Don't cry and make us feel bad. Wipe your tears and get well soon. I will come and see you tomorrow," she left, leaving her deep presence behind. I actually started feeling better. I was like, what just happened? She came in out of nowhere and left an imprint of her teary smile in my head. She kind of blessed me and disappeared after saying what she had to. It wasn't a divine intervention, but just something too human and too realistic. Some people do leave their personal battles aside to light up other people's faces. They just provide you with something that you probably didn't even know you needed. She swept the room with zest and buoyancy.

Her face and her words are deeply engraved in my mind. I salute to all such frontline healthcare workers who give away

their heart and soul to their work to leave a lasting impact on patients like me (and many more).

Grateful ✓

A week later, as there was a slight increase in my Hb levels, the doctors permitted me to go home. They were doubtful that one of my drugs, Linezolid (600 mg), was affecting the bone marrow, resulting in the low Hb levels. They slowly asked me to resume all the medicines and keep a track of CBC - (complete blood count) on a weekly basis. I came home after a week feeling slightly less disgusting. The lymph nodes which had reduced in size, slowly started to increase again. I was meticulously taking all the tablets for three months but even that seven-day gap was enough for the lethal bacteria to attack with a bang. It was then I realized how deadly the disease is. As per the doctor's suggestions I slowly started taking my TB medicines. With the constant bombardment (again) of the drugs, the swelling started shrinking. We were also keeping a track of the blood count regularly.

Two months passed, and as I said in my second chapter, I was keeping an eye on FTII, Film and Television Institute, Pune. Finally, the dates for the entrance exam were declared - 18th December, 2021. I wanted to appear for a Masters in Screen Acting program. It was the end of November. I was like, the course starts next year - in June 2022 - I can give the exam now and by the time the results come in, I will be totally fine. Also, the intensity of parosmia had slightly started to decrease. I had successfully overcome the side effects of shorter regimen and I was beating parosmia too. I knew that this cycle would soon come to an end and that everything will be great in the coming year. NO MORE BOOM! YES!!

I charged myself up and started the preparations. Exam was in mid-December, so I dedicated the rest of the days to my studies while simultaneously juggling the work at Fiction Foxx. I had also resumed a light workout after a long time. A day before my exam, as I was returning home post brisk walking, I got my weekly CBC report. The Hb levels had dropped from 10-point something to 9. I was like, *Whaaaattt?* Now that my diet was proper, I had smartly altered my diet according to parosmia. I was eating everything except onions, garlic, milk, and eggs. I had replaced these food items with some other tolerable, nutrient-rich food products. Why were the reports still so bad? Shutting down all my thoughts, I focused on my studies and left for the exam the next day. Just before leaving the house, I sensed a difficulty in wearing my shoes. Something bothered me—I had a mild tingling sensation in my feet. Also, I started having the same nauseating feeling like I had in September, when my Hb levels were 7. But I stormed out of my house without uttering a word because I didn't want anyone to stop me from going after something that I had been chasing for a long time. I went, gave my exam, smashed all the answers, and returned home, carrying my shoes in hand, feeling flushed and drained. The unwavering positivity had completely diminished. I unmasked my feelings, threw myself on the couch, and braced myself for the holiday season—intuitively knowing that it wasn't going to be as happy as I thought it would be!!!

I guess my secret Santa was already dashing through the snow—quite on its way!

#NotsoMerryChristmas

CHAPTER 6

Ouch My Feet!!!

December has always been my favorite month, not just because of the holiday vibe, but also, rather mainly, because it beautifully wraps up all the bittersweet moments of the passing year while simultaneously carrying a sense of hope for the coming year.

For me, 2021 had created a massive stir and put me on a toss that I had never imagined myself going in for. I was desperate to have better days, and I would like to believe that I was working hard under the given circumstances to make that happen. Appearing for the FTII exam was like having that one chance to change my life, and in no way I wanted to jinx it. I was feeling extremely giddy while I was on my way to the exam center. It was 18th December, 2021. The shooting pain in my feet had also started to intensify. I kept diverting my attention from both the issues that had started to bother me—the old, familiar nauseated feeling and the newly started ant crawling sensation in the feet. In the examination hall, I slipped my feet out of the shoes as the burning and tingling sensation was killing me from the inside. I was rigorously prepared and was determined to put my best foot forward, quite literally. Looking at the paper, I was more than relieved—at least on one front—because I knew the answers to 95 percent of the questions. I felt a rush in me, and I lifted my pen to effectively channel all my pain. After three hours, I was happy and slightly proud for not letting myself down. I was so sure I would be in for the next round of interviews that while coming back home, even though I felt sluggish, I imagined myself sitting in front of the panel, discussing my future ambitions. That was very kiddish of me, but can't help it. Humans are instilled with a weird sense of imagination, and I happily surrender to such fleeting moments of divine escape!! Hahh!!

So, coming back home, I did not have to explain anything to anyone. A big retching followed by a stream of vomit was enough for them to understand that something was abnormal. They were worried because they thought I was showing similar patterns after three months. Hemoglobin had already started declining. After a while, I told my parents that I feel as if someone is poking my feet with pointed needles and that it bothered me a lot, even more than the nauseated feeling. I slept over it and decided to go to the doctor. I did my CBC and was shocked to learn that the Hb levels had again dropped down to 7. Later, I realized that, in my case, feeling nauseated could be a sign of dropping Hb levels. I had these exact same patterns in September, but I had blamed it on parosmia. This time, the declining trend of hemoglobin was rapid. The level had dipped from 9.8 to 7.1 in a span of just a few days. I was immediately sent to a hematologist; he saw my entire case and asked me to get a few more tests done. Meanwhile, I was put on some extra medicines that would boost my hemoglobin. After a few days, he revealed that it was Linezolid, one of my drugs, that was causing this, since all other blood parameters were well within the normal range. He advised my TB doctors to stop the drug with immediate effect.

I limped back to the TB department and conveyed everything that the hematologist had said. Looking at my limp, the doctors asked me what was wrong. I told them about the tingling sensation in my feet, which kept on increasing with each passing day. I wasn't able to hold my slippers. After examining and questioning for several minutes, the doctors explained that my nerves were damaged due to the toxicity of the same drug. They named this condition drug-induced peripheral neuropathy. I was prescribed a tablet on a temporary basis for the pain and was asked to meet the neurologist as soon as possible.

I recalled my school days, wherein we used to play the relay races. In that, a baton was passed from one runner to the next, and so on till you reached the finish line. Standing in the hospital lobby that day, I felt like I was a baton, being passed from one department to the other, waiting to reach the finish line of this newly started relay race.

Since the appointment with the neurologist was not available for another week, I continued taking the temporarily prescribed tablet. To be honest, I did not feel any difference; the pain kept intensifying. It was on Christmas Eve that I started crying like a child. To define the exact feeling, it felt as if a barbed wire was wrapped around my feet, which kept getting tighter and tighter everyday—it burned and it ached. The pain was so excruciating that I had developed hypersensitivity; I could not even imagine anything around my feet, not even my own touch. The toes—the toe tips, to be precise—weren't able to tolerate any sort of friction. It was very cold, but I wasn't able to put on shoes, socks, or cover my feet with a blanket. The very thought of enclosing my feet or wrapping them around with a cloth was tormenting. My mother suggested that she should try massaging my feet with sesame oil and a hot bag. NOOOOO!!! I revolted. She was confused too, because on one hand, I kept telling her that I was feeling cold, but my nerves were screaming fire on the inside. Like, how should I put it?? Okay, my skin was feeling the chills, as in, 'externally', but something burned 'internally'—it was hot and cold at the same time—ABSOLUTELY MIND BOGGLING!!! It wasn't like cramps or anything that is muscular, wherein a hot bag helps in making you feel a bit better.

I shouted even when someone walked two feet away from me. On the outside, everything looked fine; nobody could tell by looking at my feet that something was wrong. But on the inside, it was a disaster which kept getting worse day by day. I was taken to the hospital on the night of 25th December by my father, my forever Santa. As a gift, I was given two back-to-back injections, one for hemoglobin and the other for nerve pain. To observe the effect of these injections, once again I was asked to stop all the TB tablets right away (hiatus from the TB drugs was actually my real Christmas gift). We left the hospital with some more of those injections, which I had to take daily for the next four days.

The thing about peripheral neuropathy is that the shooting pain increases during the night time. As I mentioned before, the ant crawling sensation intensified, making my legs heavy, numb, and *unmovable,* so naturally, my nights were sleepless. I finished the four-day course of those injections without feeling any better. On the night of 30th December, I sensed a different kind of pain. By this time, the tingling sensation had already gone up to my knees. I was lying on my bed, half covered in a blanket, when an electric shock-like sensation ran from my toes to my head. Imagine someone giving you an electric shock. How would your body react? I was popping like popcorn!! This current-like thing was acting in rounds—one toe at a time. Once all 10 toes were done, it would start again and keep repeating. My toenails were severely hurting. OUCH MY FEEEEET... I shrieked every time the sensation ran in my body. It was impossible to divert my attention. I tried listening to podcasts or even tried relaxing by watching *Friends,* BUT NOTHING WORKED! How was I possibly going to not let an electric shock or a live wire-like feeling affect me? I could actually sense something traveling its way up from toe - right to the head. I breathed heavily to calm myself down. I was exhausted, sweating like a pig on a chilly night! After six hours, somewhere around five in the morning, these rounds stopped (but the pain still continued), and I slept!!

I woke up in the morning, telling my parents about this scary episode. The speed with which the pain kept intensifying was just scary. It was absolutely impossible for me to touch my feet on the ground. In the evening (yea, 31st December, New Year's Eve), we went to the hospital again. Before going there, we had simple plans: my sister was going to make 'parosmia-friendly misal' for me without any onion or garlic (I salute her skills!!), and the four of us were going to welcome the coming year, 2022, in a low-key fashion!! But going to the hospital crushed all our plans. I limped inside the doctor's cabin wearing my toilet slippers (the one which has a joint between your first and second toes for a better grip) because I couldn't wear anything else. I did not allow the doctor to check my feet. I screamed as he started walking near me. The hypersensitivity had increased. Seeing the worsened condition of my feet, he mentioned in my file that I had progressed from having 'drug-induced peripheral neuropathy' to 'drug-induced *severe* peripheral neuropathy'. The TB drugs were still on hold. The nurse put me in a wheelchair and took me to the second-floor deluxe room. I was given a good spot near a huge window from where I was going to see the light of 2022. TADAAAA… I was hospitalized. I couldn't help but notice the contrast between last year's 31st and the present day, where the only shots I was going to have were those of injections!!

At night, I was sitting by the hospital window to see the firecrackers as everyone bade goodbye to the passing year. It was a view I can never forget. Against the backdrop of a sky filled with colors, the highway looked beautiful. It was such an irony. People were screaming. Well, so was I, but our reasons were completely opposite, thanks to the same 'current episode' which had already kicked in. I never imagined I would embrace the new year like this. It was for the first time in my life, I realized that 31st December is not about celebration for everyone. There are some who suffer while we all party and have a gala time. My sister was there, nervously trying to cheer me up with her jokes. Later, as the stabbing sensation got unbearable, she called the nurse, who then called the doctor. I was given an injection for the pain, but it did not subside whatsoever. Around 2 p.m., the nurse came again to give me another shot of a painkiller, followed by a sleep-inducing tablet. But guess what? Nothing worked. After a while, I was tired of bothering people. It was already new year's night. I was feeling awful for making my sister spend it in the hospital. I didn't want to put her into this with me yet again. The first time I was hospitalized was her birthday, 26th September. She had left her birthday celebration after hearing about my hospitalization and even on 31st December, she was standing strong by my side. Today we casually joke that I had chosen the *perfect* days both times to get hospitalized - her birthday and New Year's Eve.

With a tinge of guilt taking over, I rolled over to the other side of the bed, pretending I was asleep, trying to tolerate the pain while shedding a muffled cry. I was so pissed! It's a night I can never forget. I was angry, frustrated, resentful, and helpless; felt bitter about feeling bitter.

The pain (yes, the word PAIN is repetitive, but I officially give up the search for synonyms on thesaurus; let's just use the word as it is) was just a trigger to so many things that I had been suppressing all those months. I was 24. I didn't want to spend my days like this in a hospital. Exposing my vulnerability by typing this out seems scary, but yes, I was feeling left out. People my age were traveling the world, earning money, spending money, and chasing competitive careers. What was I doing?? Sobbing on a hospital bed?? Popping pills like an elderly person? Taking injections every now and then?? I recalled the saying; *I am too young to be this old!!!*

I didn't want to 'celebrate' but I didn't want to spend my night like that either.

It was for the first time in all those months I felt, WHY ME???

I quickly recognized that I was going down a nasty road. Having always looked up to my mother, who has involuntarily taught me the value of not giving up, it was deeply carved in my head that one must be 'realistically strong' (will expand on this in the coming chapters) in the tough times and not let that phase get the worst of you. I felt a bit ashamed of myself for having this pity party, and wiped my eyes. "Your mother is a tigress; stop crying," I kept telling myself. But the tears did not stop. Later, I realized that I was crying *because* I was crying. Silly me! My reaction to every overwhelming emotion is to cry!!! I acknowledged that I was feeling bad but tried not to let it go out of my hands. I tightened my fists as the current/shock episode hit the crescendo. After an hour, as the sun rose, I finally went to sleep.

I woke up as the housekeeping lady came in to change my sheets. It was around 7 a.m. With all the hassle around, even my sister woke up. Rather than resting for five minutes more, we decided to start our day. She handed me a toothbrush as I sat on my bed. Since one of my hands was tied to a saline bottle, she helped me comb my hair. Meanwhile, she also turned the hot water tap on for me to have my bath. I rested my arm on my sister's shoulder and balanced myself on the edges of my heel. I went inside the washroom but felt useless. The whole point of having a shower was to feel fresh, neat, and hygienic, but it was going to be incomplete without cleaning off my feet, which were extremely dirty as I had not touched them since neuropathy had started. I felt like taking a scrub and brushing them rigorously, but in reality, I couldn't even wash them with simple water. I have been very obsessive about having my feet clean. I used to scrub them, moisturize them, and wear slippers in the house to keep them exceptionally sparkly. But it was a long time since I had taken care of them, and I felt pathetic about it. I was someone who used to wear socks in dirty places to make sure that the dust did not stick to my skin, and there I was walking barefoot with absolutely filthy, greasy, and unwashed feet. *Blahhhhhh...even typing this out makes me cringe!!*

I was out of the shower, feeling not so *freshy freshy*! My sister instantly got a bottle of rose water from her 'huge kit' (I would have to write another book on that) and sprayed it on my face. Well, I don't know about the rose water, but the fact that my sister's solution to every problem lies in her 'kit' made me grin and eventually progress to smiling ear to ear. After tidying me up, she made me sit under the warm sunlight near the window and insisted on clicking my picture to put on our family group. She did her job and left the hospital to get me some breakfast! GOD! I JUST LOVE HER!

Both times, in September and December, I was admitted to hospital XYZ (can't take the name, but it is owned by the same surgeon who had done my mother's cancer surgeries and my initial diagnosis of TB). Since he is an extremely respected and trustworthy doctor who knew my line of treatment, he communicated with my TB doctors at the government hospital and kept them in loop. On 3rd January, since it was Saturday and Sunday in between, he sent us to the government hospital to meet the HOD of the TB ward and officially stop the drug Linezolid. I wasn't formally discharged from the hospital, and hence the scalp vein was still on my wrist. It was just wrapped around with a bandage to make it look less obvious. I was put on a wheelchair, and both my parents drove me off to the government hospital. Seeing me in a wheelchair, the team of doctors quickly took me inside the follow-up room. Stopping Linezolid was going to be a huge step. It was toxic (for me), but it was and still is an effective anti-TB drug used for MDR treatment. The doctors had to come up with an alternative drug that would compensate for the stopped drug. The HOD was yet to come in the picture. By then, his equally efficient team was preparing for a new combination of treatments. They were discussing whether or not they should get me injectable drugs. One of the doctors told me that I might have to start taking the injections daily for the next six months. I panicked, for I knew that injections were even more hazardous. In some cases, they caused permanent hearing loss. Seeing my concern, the staff casually said that wearing hearing aids is as normal as wearing specs (yes, I have specs) and that I should normalize it in case the hearing loss happens. I just freaked out. I was already suffering from various side effects of the drugs, and in the case of injections, the side effects were obvious and commonly seen in many survivors. I panicked. I didn't want to compromise my hearing. Four out of my five senses were already hampered in the past few months: I had blurry vision, distorted sense of smell and taste due to parosmia and then neuropathy had wrecked my sense of touch. My ears were still thankfully working in condition and I was not ready to lose my only functioning sense organ. My parents were scared too. My dad, being extremely sensitive, was ready to pick a fight, if needed. He just wanted his daughter to be alright—out of that damn wheelchair as soon as possible!!

Getting to meet the HOD was our only hope. He finally arrived and examined my overall health. The nerves were damaged to a great extent. He insisted on meeting the neurologist as soon as possible, because the specialist could provide a better take on my condition and prescribe tests and tablets that would help in subsiding the severe pain. Apart from that, he said that my overall progress with TB has been great—the lymph nodes had fully disappeared, and my weight too was fine. He said that I need not take any injectable drugs. Getting a Bedaquiline (a drug that I had already taken without observing any side effects for the first six months of my treatment) extension for another six months would serve the purpose. Healing neuropathy would take a lot of time, he said, but leaving that aspect aside, my TB recovery was excellent. However, to get an extension, we needed to submit an official letter to the main TB hospital in Sewri, Mumbai. I needed to accompany my parents there, as the hospital staff in Sewri needed to check the patient before altering the course of treatment. We did that the next day.

Stepping into the main TB hospital in Sewri gave me a reality check. I could faintly see patients across the spectrum—good, better, and worse!! The multi-story building was just packed with TB patients from different areas. All of this pointed towards a disturbing truth: We have TB cases more than we think we know. We don't really talk about the disease the way we are supposed to! The hush-hush around the topic is just strengthening the taboo. PATIENTS SUFFER MORE BECAUSE OF THE IGNORANCE. PERIOD!

Seeing the young, the middle-aged, and the old patients walk around helplessly was simply heart-rending. While leaving the hospital, a peon, roughly my father's age, came near my wheelchair. He had genuinely helped us with the formalities and paperwork. All my father could do was offer him some amount, as a way of saying thank you. He respectfully declined the offer and instead tapped me on my head. He said that I was too young to be on a wheelchair. All he wished was for me to have a very bright future. He asked me to be strong and healthy. I could sense his voice getting heavy. I was silenced. I just joined my hands and extended my gratitude!! This was my second experience with the health workers hitting me hard with their kindness and dedication. I am extremely grateful to have collected such pearls of humanity that humble me as a person. Yes, money can't buy everything. I hope my silence was loud enough that day!

I came back and got myself re-hospitalized after a long, disturbing, yet grounding day. The neurologist was requested to pay a personal visit to the hospital, and he was kind enough to accept that. He came in at night, when the shock episode had begun; therefore, he actually got to see what really bothered me. I screamed as he came near me with a T-shaped metallic instrument, so he dropped the hammer-like thing but examined my feet anyway. I kept shouting as he checked my feet in different places. After several minutes, he re-confirmed what we already knew. Linezolid had wrecked my nerves to a great extent. I would not be able to regain my sense of touch for a *very* long time, he said. I begged him to give me something that would make the shock sensation go away. I just wanted to sleep better. He was empathetic, but he was realistic too. He explained that the damage was too much, plus I was already on the treatment for TB, so it is possible that the existing drugs hinder my progress. He prescribed a strong dose of various antidepressants that would put a slow end to the active-shock-like pain at night; however, warned us that the stabbing sensation would continue during the day for a while. Nerve regeneration is a long process, so getting back to normal would take time—several months or even years. He painted a realistic picture without sounding scary and wished me luck for a speedy recovery!! Just after he left, my sister got the prescribed medicines.

Antidepressants? Really?

I never thought I would have to take them!

Yes, it was a long road ahead—a road that I wasn't supposed to encounter at all; neuropathy wasn't supposed to erupt; antidepressants weren't supposed to be a part of my TB treatment. But whatever it was, it was getting me ready to walk the *road less traveled, because that was going to make all the difference!*

#WillBeBackOnMyFeet

CHAPTER 7

Living With Neuropathy

I took the anti-depressants along with some vitamin tablets that the neurologist had prescribed. He had also given me a gel that I was supposed to apply on my feet to numb the sensation. I just wanted to get rid of the pain, so I squeezed the tube really hard and took out a large amount of gel. I was scared to touch my feet, but I hesitantly applied the gel on my toe tips and made a thick layer of it. I thought, "Now I will be pain-free, yesss!!"

But as soon as it dried, it became sticky and heavy. The thick layer was cracking up, and my toes started feeling 'more stretchy'. MORE GEL, MORE RELIEF was a silly thought, and I realized I had made a blunder. I took a wet tissue and started wiping it. It was around 12 in the night. I was hitting every possible (not-so) musical note while screaming. Finally, after relentless efforts, I was able to wipe off the gel. Looking at my greasy feet, I was tempted to clean them off too, but honestly, I had no guts left. I brushed aside my temptations and took the wet tissue box out of my sight. But then, I suddenly had an *aha* moment. I was so indulged in the gel fiasco; I hadn't noticed that the shock episode had stopped. Stopped, like literally!! I mean, I still felt the stabbing sensation, but I was glad that I wasn't popping like popcorn anymore. After a long stretch of sleepless nights, I was excited to roll back on my bed.

Next day, I must have woken up around nine. I still felt drowsy. The antidepressants were so heavy that it was difficult for me to open my eyes. Well, I didn't mind that; the neurologist had already told me about the possible side effects of the antidepressants, like feeling drowsy or feeling too hungry. I guess by that time I was smart enough to understand and come to terms with the fact that having medicines is like a chain reaction. It cures one thing by affecting some other thing!

I was taking medicines (the antidepressants) having side effects for the side effects caused by other medicines (the TB drugs)!

Five days later, still in the hospital, I tried getting out of the wheelchair. Very slowly… I started practicing my walk. It was painful. My feet were puffy due to the swelling. Now I was holding onto someone's hand rather than leaning on their shoulder completely.

A week later, I was resting in my room when the doctor and his team came in for the rounds. I was all alone. They asked me to stand up and walk towards them. I was stumped. Not that I was scared of falling or tripping, but I felt like it was a test I had to pass. I didn't want to look like a fool in front of *all* of them. I stood up and took the support of the bed. "No," he said, "leave that and see if you can do it by yourself." I got rid of the support and balanced myself on the edges of my feet. I shrieked, but now I was too proud to give up. I took two-three baby steps, and the doctors seemed satisfied. But I hadn't finished yet. Looking at their faces, I pulled myself back, took a deep breath, and finished the remaining steps in one go. The nurse gave me her hand as I stumbled upon her. I looked at the doctor like a preschool kid, waiting to get a gold star. "Very well. You look better. We can let you go home," he said. I *sooo* wanted to jump and express my relief, but instead all I could do was just dip my knees in excitement—that was my jump *without a jump*!

My father came in to complete the discharge formality. I had to change my clothes. Thankfully, my mother had sent a pair of 'wide-legged pants'. The very idea of wearing tights or skinny jeans was like a nightmare! I could not have let the long fabric rub against my toes because of the hypersensitivity. Friction was still a big problem. Since the pants were wide, I could easily (yet cautiously) glide my feet through them. The next task was wearing the footwear. I took a slipper in my hand, stretched its belt, and slowly slid my foot in it. I repeated the same with my next foot, and voila! I was ready to go!!!

Coming home after a year felt amazing, considering I had left the house on December 31st. After being back, I had to plan my routine according to the new medicines. I was sleeping for more than 18 hours and was eating like a hog. I used to have my breakfast twice in the morning. I was having two large *puran polis* - a Maharashtrian sweet dish, just as a *light* snack. I never had a sweet tooth, but in that phase, I was sweeping everything off my plate—the sweets, the savory…EVERYTHING! I was a personified version of Eat, Sleep, Repeat

For almost one week after coming home, I had terrible sleepless nights. I used to have nightmares and chills, and my legs used to get heavy. Imagine thousands of ants—the big ones—crawling and biting all over your legs! This is the closest parallel I can draw while explaining how I used to feel. At times, in the middle of the night, I have sat upright and brushed my legs, thinking that those ants might actually go away. Silly! But I was very unlike myself. I don't know why!

A few days later, I started observing tingling sensations even in my hands. I thought that my hands would have the same fate as my feet. I was nervous, but I was scared to tell my parents. I didn't want them to worry. Later, I confronted them anyway, and thankfully, the existing antidepressants prevented any further damage. Also, I observed a tiny cyst below the left side of my ear. It was smaller as compared to what I had got in the beginning, but this time it had attacked a new place—the left side instead of the right side. For almost 20 days, my TB medicines were on hold. I knew I had to restart my regular dose. So without really waiting for the doctors to give me a green signal in person, I decided to start taking the TB drugs after seeking their advice over a phone call.

Every time I underestimate the disease or its treatment, I get my lesson. Starting the TB medicines after almost 20 days was again a problem. I was taking these tablets for almost seven months. But a 20-day gap was enough for the body to forget what it was bombarded with. However, in order to start the TB tablets, I had to make a timetable because now I was taking a range of medicines, allopathy for TB and neuropathy and an additional course of homeopathy medicines for overall immunity.

This is how my schedule looked:

9 a.m.: Two antidepressants and two vitamins
9.30 am - Homeopathy
10 a.m. to 1 p.m.: Eight TB tablets at regular intervals of half an hour
1.30 pm: Vitamin B12 and a syrup
2 p.m.: Homeopathy
8 p.m.: Two antidepressants and four vitamins
8.30 pm – Homeopathy

...and these were the only hours that I used to be awake. Rest of the time, I was in a deep sleep. I decided to quit my job at Fiction Foxx because it was really tough to stay awake and concentrate after taking high doses of antidepressants.

As the weeks passed, I touched my entire foot to the ground. It was all cushiony due to the swelling. With very gradual improvement—after falling and failing—I slowly dared to massage my sole with some oils. I couldn't recognize any touch with my eyes closed, as in, I could understand that I was touching my toes, but *I couldn't feel which toe* I was touching.

In the days that followed later, I ordered a baby tooth brush—the one with feathery bristles—for cleaning my feet. The day I washed them with lots of foam... It was painful, but the joy was unmatchable. I was just a few washes away from getting sparkling feet!! Yayy!

Cleaning my feet regularly was ticked off my list, but I was still unable to wear and hold slippers at home. The toes had become too fragile to hold anything properly. I started hunting for exercises on YouTube that could strengthen my toes. No way I was going to sit back and just wait for the medicines to cure my nerve pain. It was extremely difficult to perform those exercises in the beginning, but brick by brick, one day at a time, with consistent efforts, I managed to walk by myself.

Two months later, somewhere in March, we went to see the doctor. Now that I was able to walk on my own, the doctors asked me to slowly taper the dose of antidepressants. He also warned me about the withdrawals that would follow after stopping the antidepressants. I was prepared. I knew that the very first problem that would present itself would be in the form of insomnia. I started tapering the dose, and one by one, the withdrawal symptoms came knocking through my doors.

Firstly, it was insomnia, as expected. I was caught up between scanty sleep and disturbing vivid dreams. I was awake and not awake at the same time. Every time someone tried waking me up, I was all scared and drenched in sweat.

Secondly, my eyes and ears became sensitive to light and sound, respectively. I avoided talking to anyone in person or even on a call and preferred sitting alone in the room with the drapes shut.

Thirdly, my appetite was killed. My stomach used to ache, and I was throwing up like before.

Fourthly, I was feeling gloomy all day.

And last, but not the least, the mood swings. They were so terrible. I literally used to cry for days, and I am not exaggerating at all. It was so loud that, forget my family, I was scared of myself. I was not a pleasant person to be around.

The withdrawals lasted for more than a month. Since I had no idea about the severity of withdrawals, I had taken up new work assignments. I was working for an audiobook company and was recording books in my voice, just by sitting at home. It required me to sit and record for more than eight hours a day. Because of the withdrawals, the work was hampered. I was a mess and was not in a state to listen to my own voice. I hate giving excuses at work, so I kept doing my job until it backfired. Knowing that I would not be able to meet the deadlines, I asked the company people to replace me. But they were kind enough to extend the deadlines. I was grateful, but I was also fed up with being caught in a vicious cycle. I wanted to feel normal and have a decent job to keep myself occupied. I decided to break through it.

I started asking people about how to overcome the withdrawal symptoms. I learned that working out would help me get rid of the toxins. I decided to resume my workout. But how was I going to do it? I had literally no clue where to begin considering the increased pain that had followed after stopping the antidepressants. I still knew I had to find a way. With joint pain being my all-time companion since the treatment, a gym workout was out of question. The safest possible exercise was going to be Surya Namaskar, the Sun Salutation. I took my yoga mat, dusted it off, and laid it on the floor. I changed my clothes, stood on the mat, and took the first pose, then the next, until I reached *Dandasana* - a plank pose where you curl your toes outwards, and boom...I fell on the ground. The toes were so rigid that it was almost impossible to get ahead. I was already fuming with rage. I was ready to fall 10 more times, but I sure as hell wanted to complete at least one round of the namaskar. I told myself that it's just a matter of going past that initial pain. I was so determined to sweat everything out that I stood up, went back to pose one, and fell again and again and again until I was done with the last, 12th pose.

I dabbed my sweat and pulled off some more stretches. I tried channeling my anger in a way that would pay me back and ease my withdrawals. I was forcing myself to come back to my original form. The body was yearning for dopamine??? Well, I was going to give it some!!

I completed my workout session feeling slammed and exhausted. I lied on the mat, caught my breath, and realized that my toes were all sore. I stood up and stared at my sweaty body in the mirror. I looked myself in the eye, and I liked what I saw. I was crying, but it was accompanied by sheer determination and an unwillingness to give up. I swear, I loved myself more than anyone else that day. 'Yes, pain and resilience go hand in hand.' I cheered myself and took on the challenge of transitioning myself from abnormal to FABnormal!!! I was ready (?) for the next thing that was waiting for me ahead!

#ExpectTheUnexpected

CHAPTER 8

Bitter Ending or Better Beginning?

I have reiterated time and again that TB treatment was just a catalyst in changing so many things in my life. My professional life was already at stake because I had chosen a career wherein if you are out of sight, you are out of mind. I am sure the people with whom I had worked in the past had simply forgotten that I existed—and why not? I never held any grudges because I thought my personal life was far more comforting. But clearly, it was all a hoax!

Seven chapters down, and this is the hardest thing to write!

Throughout the book, I have mentioned about my parents and my sister; no other aspect of my personal life has been highlighted in the previous pages, and I never would have! But somewhere in the beginning, I have said that I was fine with everything that was happening in my life because of the treatment, until my people—*all of them*—had my back. Apart from my family, there was one more person whom I had strongly counted on. Never thought he would leave my hand—not in this phase and definitely not after six years of 'being together'. There is no point in pretending we don't know whom I am talking about. Let's just call him X. Yes, pun intended!

I did briefly mention him in the second chapter, where I have written about the dichotomy of 9th January in my life. It was his mother. I was 18 when he and I first met, and no way will I ever think of it as a passing affair, because six and a half years is definitely a long time!

He flew abroad three months after I started my medications. He had seen me in my horrible state, and hence, he was hesitant to leave me behind. But I had my family, so I did encourage him to go ahead and pursue his and his late mother's dreams. Having a relationship in different time zones was going to be a tedious thing, but I had my priorities straight! HE IS THE ONE. PERIOD. It doesn't matter how far he is; he will always be my... whatever! But sadly, things change. People change!

One fine day, in May 2022, shortly after my 25th birthday, he told me out of the blue, Let's take a break. Let's not talk for a few days—days which eventually turned into months! No explanation whatsoever! I tried asking him if there's anything that's bothering him there. Why does he want to stop talking, and how is that going to be a solution to whatever that he was dealing with? I was ready to help him, but was he ready to help me? I don't know!

After that phone call, I immediately recalled our three-week-old conversation. He had asked me if I was feeling under confident. He knew about the withdrawals, yes! But he said that I seemed off and wanted to know if I was really okay.

Honestly, I had not asked myself that question before. I was dealing with an enormous emotional shift, but I had never looked at myself with an objective eye. I knew that tablets take a toll on a patient's mental health—something that is not being discussed widely—but I was deliberately trying not to talk about it because that would have lowered my morale even more. Yes, I used to cry easily. I felt overwhelmed, anxious, nervous, tired, helpless, and so many things that I could not even articulate. But I never really bothered him with my worries (I mean, I would like to believe so). So, when he asked me if I was dealing with low self-esteem, I just burst out. I started crying and told him that I cannot understand whether it's me or the medicines. I explained that everything seemed uncertain. I feared that I was home for almost two years, and maybe that's making me feel as if I am lagging behind. I wasn't feeling sorry for myself, but I was feeling left out. I was feeling despondent. He patiently listened to all that I had to say. Then he politely asked me not to worry and said that everything will be fine. He assured me that it's all going to work out and that he was proud of me for pulling it through. He boosted my confidence by saying that it's a tough phase and that I needed to stay put. And I did!

Merely 20 days after this conversation, the contrasting words that came marching out of his mouth blew me away completely. Was he hinting something? Did my vulnerability throw him off? I just wanted to know why he was taking such an extreme step? WHY?? And plus, what ramifications would the 'not talking' phase have on 'our' future? I could sense where we were leading, but I never dared to say anything out loud. Eventually, after months, the thing that I was the most scared of manifested itself.

He dropped the massive bomb! He left me out high and dry! He parted ways!

So, without dwelling too much into the hows and whys of him abandoning me during my worst (he has his reasons, I am sure), I will get straight to the point... because this ain't about him... This is about me, and no way there is a room in here for any *exes*. I mean excess!

I know I was deeply hurt, shattered to my core, for this was my worst nightmare. I have always been a strong girl, but yeah, I accept that this was my ugliest and scariest *boom* ever. This relationship was everything that I had ever dreamed of. Our relationship was upheld as sacrosanct (just by me?). It was too good to have such a dirty and abrupt end. I wanted him; I really did. How could a guy like him take such an extreme step? What made him do that? All of this coming from him was truly a shocker. I cried, questioned my worth, blamed myself for being on a sabbatical, and hated myself.

"Why did he do this? How come there can be no explanation? Do I not deserve one? Is it because I am sick? Does it make me worthless? Is he ashamed of me? Does he never think about me? Did he never care at all? What about the promises that he made before he left? What about him not leaving my hand at the airport? Did I miss out the subtle hints when he stopped video calling days after going abroad? Was I so naive when I thought I should give him space to adjust in a new country? Was I stupid to trust him blindly? Was I waiting for nothing? Was it foolish of me to miss him in the hospital and not tell him about it, thinking he would be worried? Was it just me??....... Was I this? Was I that?? STOPPPPP IT"

I realized that I was sinking! I spent EVERY SINGLE NIGHT shedding silent tears and asking myself the same questions over and over again for months! I was not ready to accept that one can give closure (over a phone call) to something that lasted for more than six years. NO NO NO! A BIG NO!! My head kept spinning!

I am a perpetual overthinker who easily gets into a shell. I never really followed up *toooo* much on him after that last phone call (I must have made a maximum of five calls in the next six months, that's it!). I was simply wrapped up in my own thoughts. I blamed TB for making me hit rock bottom...for making me indulge in self-loathing! I was tired of making quick runs to the washroom and dealing with the unpredictable anxiety attacks—BREATHE IN-EXHALE-BREATHE IN. No, not working!

Waking up daily feeling heavy and unenthusiastic was not a pleasant routine. I hated everything. My self-esteem was just crushed. Can you fathom how torturous it is to feel rejected? Especially when you are already at the edge of a cliff? I felt insulted, I was hurt, I was angry, and the worst part is I never really vented it properly. I wanted out! Yes, time heals everything, but I was so desperate to drag myself out of the chaos... to get rid of the self-harming thoughts that 'one day at a time' wasn't just working for me in this phase. I wanted more. How and where was I possibly going to find it?

I was sent to the darkest of places after the heartbreak (hate this word, though). No clarity about career, no clarity about personal life, and lastly, no clarity about how and when to share all of this with my parents! I looked happy, but I wasn't.

I had put on a show. I am pouring this piece of information here because I kept hiding it from people. I carried the burden of a 'failed relationship' and allowed it to label me as a 'failure'. This is my attempt to come out and get rid of the shame and guilt, which are not mine to hold. Also, sadly, I have come across so many women whose marriages were called off due to them being TB patients. I absolutely detest such families, husbands, or fiancés who abandon their own person during such physical, mental and emotional hardships. SHAME! (In my case, the relationship didn't come to an end because of my sickness; he deserves some credit!).

Even though I am an emotional fool, I am also a problem solver. I do not like sulking. Even during my hospitalizations or the painful phases of physical complications, I always came up with a plan instead of stinking in a dingy place. I am always up for finding solutions, rather than sitting in a puddle of problems. I was ready to do anything that would detach me from the gut-wrenching, mind-numbing, or nerve-racking (whatever you wish to call it) reality.

I knew I was on tablets that trigger anxiety, induce depression, and basically mess with your mental health in ways that one cannot even think of. In retrospect, I feel I should have sought help. One more mistake, and I wish others would avoid it.

I was centering myself and making sure that I do not fall prey to any of the side effects that escalated my trauma. I had to do *something*. Nothing changes if nothing changes, right? Even though I hated going one day at a time, going one day at a time was the only option. It was silly of me to expect that

I would magically feel fine one morning! I had to start small, brick by brick!

I needed to 'process'…but before that, I needed to 'accept'. While fixating over the WHY part, I told myself that everything happens for a reason. What if I was meant to rediscover myself? Maybe all bad things coming together at the same time could be God's way of testing me, and being a nerd, I had to pass the test with flying colors. It was almost like erasing my past, focusing on my present, and reinventing my future.

I had to pick myself up, and while doing so, I had to be realistically strong, meaning I allowed myself to have bad days, cry it out, and get done with it. It is unreal to feel positive at all times. Rather, I feel setting such goals leads to more disappointment and frustration. Healing is never linear, said Jennifer Lawrence in one of her interviews, and I completely resonate with it. Having that larger bandwidth takes a lot off your plate. I decided to cut myself some slack and just focus on making the present day as happy as possible.

Before the onset of this gigantic emotional wave, healing for me was just physical. I was obsessed with getting my body right. I never considered that I would ever be an emotional mess. Now that it had happened, I had to gather myself. But looking back, I feel it was during these times that I learned some of my best lessons. Well, what doesn't break you makes you stronger.

It was time to grow. It was time to let go, and letting go takes work. Plus, what's healing without dealing with that sh***y feeling? After popping so many pills, the universe was preparing me to swallow the hardest 'pil' ever!

#iykyk

THE WAXING

"You have to know what sparks the light in you so that you, in your own way, can illuminate the world."

– Oprah Winfrey

CHAPTER 9

Grounding Myself

The second half of this book is not just restricted to TB. It rather deals with broader things that I have come to realize about myself and my life in general. It is about reflection, about the tools that I found, developed, and heavily relied on in the last two years. This isn't a typical guidebook that one must swear by during tough times; it's not! This is more like an effort to deconstruct and declutter the feelings, or chaos, to be more precise, that I had stashed in the shelf of my mind for a very long time.

With the onset of the pandemic, everything became distorted. So much had changed in the years that I had lost a sense of self. However, it was the ending of a relationship that triggered my existential crisis, made me question my own existence, and it robbed me of my sanity and ability to think objectively. Maybe there is a larger purpose to all of this, and I am still trying to figure out what that purpose could be. I kept going back, thinking how my life would have been if I had not had TB! A wave of anxiety took me in its arms when I sat with my own thoughts. I kept spiraling into the same dirty hole. I wasn't really liking my company. Wrapped in vulnerability and uncertainty, I had to find out who 'I' was and what 'I' wanted. With sudden disorientation, nothing felt concrete. Every day was pretty much the same: get up, take tablets, eat, have silent emotional outbursts, and go to bed. I kept feeling small and insignificant. I had come down to an absolute zero in my personal and my professional life. Earlier, I was okay with having a restart in professional life because I had the strong backing of all my loved ones. But with him suddenly leaving my side during my temporal low made everything a bit more overwhelming. It amplified the emptiness and the voice in my head: *Am I good enough?*

I wanted to prove myself by being good at something. But what? I wasn't able to step out and audition. "Who am I if not an actor? Should I change my passion? Is it possible?" I was so anchored to the notion of being an actress that not being able to act made me feel worthless. The questions kept haunting me. Everything had to be started from scratch. Some serious 'soul searching' was required to end this sh*t show, and for that, I had to be comfortable with feeling uncomfortable.

TOOL 1: JOURNALING

One way to do so was to journal my thoughts—just put everything on a piece of paper and get it out of my system. I had read about the benefits of journaling and free writing. It was very hard in the beginning. I felt like it's doing me more harm than good because every time I penned down something, it felt like replaying and reliving those tough moments, but I still adhered to it. I was never the kind of a person who indulged in making lists. But then I started making extensive lists about what it is that I want, what are my fears, what are my strengths, what are my drawbacks, and lastly, what is it that is going to make me happy—genuinely happy! As I started practicing it meticulously, I realized that I was able to articulate my thoughts, meaning that before journaling, the feelings or thoughts did not exist singularly; one thought used to beget another negative thought, thus starting a never-ending chain reaction. I used to find it extremely jarring. Now that I was putting them down on a piece of paper, I was able to peel different layers one by one. Although journaling seemed trivial at first, physicalizing the mess in my head was making me see things clearly. I was taking away the power of those thoughts. I could actually see the benefits; I could see how I evolved over a period of time. What felt taxing a few months ago was something that didn't even bother me later. The documentation helped me track my progress over the years, and now it is something that I follow 'almost' religiously, if not regularly. I am striving to be better at it; I need more consistency and discipline. But I am trying! Also, yes, it is the same habit of journaling my thoughts that led me towards the idea of writing this book. See, good things do happen! Don't they?

TOOL 2: DRIVING, HOLDING THE REINS!

I was so consumed thinking that my disease defined me and that it was responsible for everything that I had lost, including my self-confidence! Had someone asked me back then, I may not have agreed, but today I do realize that I was probably becoming president of the pity party campaign. Part of it came from the fact that I was being overprotected. Given the complexities and difficulties that I physically went through, naturally, my parents, especially my father, carried an air of constant worry and concern. I found that extremely uncomfortable. It reinforced my dependency—both physical and emotional! Either my father was dropping me to the places where I wanted to go or I had to rely on cab services; either way, I was dependent on 'someone else'. I felt like taking some charge and reiterating my self-sufficiency. So, my next step was to take the reins in my control, and driving was the way to do it (I always associated driving with being tough and independent). I told my father that I wanted to learn how to drive. I knew that neuropathy would make it very difficult—I did not have enough strength in my feet, and I was limping occasionally—but I wanted to do it anyway. I enrolled myself for a driving class, and then, quite literally, I was in the driver's seat.

The first time I held the steering wheel in my hands, aah! The joy was otherworldly! However, my driving teacher ensured that the joy didn't last for long. He kept giving instructions that I was finding difficult to process and execute: *lower the speed by applying brakes, then press the clutch, then change the gears (without looking down); also, honk to alert the pedestrians; give an indicator; use the wiper; and look in the rearview mirror—all* of it at the same time! HUH... WHAT???? I was baffled and perplexed.

During my initial days, I was picking up things *very* slowly. I remember, on my third day of the class, I had almost dashed the four-wheeler onto a tree, and when I did that, I instantly raised my hands, surrendering to my teacher, who was even more furious after seeing me leave the steering. I used to think that I was being punished, but that day, after seeing me give him a hard time, I realized that my poor teacher was at the suffering end. He may never have had such a slow student. In my defense, I told him later that I had neuropathy and that I found it difficult to sense where my foot was—

whether it was on accelerator or on a brake (looking back, I realize how risky that was). Seeing my pattern, he asked my father to additionally take my driving lessons. My father agreed! We knew it was a long way ahead. Dad started taking me daily for 45 minutes on barren roads. He knew that I was scared to go wrong, and that is exactly where I was going wrong. Yes, I received enormous scoldings from my father, but no way either of us was willing to give up. I started figuring out ways to improve my sense of touch, and for that, I started driving without wearing any footwear. I had to calm down and tell myself that I was going to do it alright. Just like journaling, where I was articulating one thought at a time, while driving, I had to process one command at a time. It was complex, but it wasn't impossible. Every single day was a revelation. I also became more observant. I was silently observing other drivers and taking mental notes to inch towards my desired goal.

I was learning something new and exciting. Falling and failing was a part of it, but I thoroughly enjoyed this patience-testing process. Finally, on 19th September, 2022 I cleared my driving test, and a few weeks later, I got my license. It was tough, but it was definitely worth it! One thing that driving taught me is that, no matter how many people accompany you, you cannot go anywhere unless 'you' twist the ignition key. Start small but start! I had successfully laid the first brick towards taking my power back—I started gaining my self-confidence! Yes!!!

TOOL 3: MINDFULNESS

Coming on to the third tool, meditation, it was and still is something that I follow consistently. My meditation practice is a mix of OM chanting and breathwork. While writing about meditation, I cannot help but mention my teacher, Mansi Gokhale, who is very generous and has been teaching OM chanting for over 20 years *without charging a penny.* She learned the technique from her Guru, Late Dr. Jayant Karandikar, who had designed a half-hour syllabus which consisted of different forms of chanting OM. It also has various syllables, like *ka, kha, ga, gha,* and so on, which, if pronounced along with OM, target the seven chakras in our body. The syllabus is a beautiful amalgamation of mind, body, and soul healing. I started taking lessons with her in 2020, just before the pandemic. At that time, my intention behind learning OM chanting was just to improve my voice (not that I am a singer, but being a theater practitioner, I felt her syllabus was an excellent *riyaz* for voice). My mother, my sister, and I were her regular students. While teaching, she used to share many success stories of people who battled life-threatening diseases and gloriously fought their way out. Of course, all of those people were taking their treatment along with practicing chakra meditation and OM chanting. All my doubts (I never had any, but still) were settled when I saw my mother come out so beautifully of her cancer phase. Even during her rough chemo days, she kept chanting. It was strange yet revealing to observe the power that OM carries.

Later, I got my firsthand experience. Initially, when I was diagnosed with MDR, I started wondering how come I had TB! I was chanting regularly and never missed a day. But as months passed, the pace at which my body was healing, not to mention the glow that never diminished, made people wonder if I was really a TB patient. Even in the hospital, I have had so many encounters wherein people were not ready to believe that I had MDR because I 'looked' well! Maybe I was meant to have TB, but after seeing other patients who unfortunately had become emaciated (I had briefly touched that phase and bounced back), I feel the severity of it was a lot more in control because of the healthy practices that I followed. All thanks to my teacher. Unfortunately, she doesn't take any online classes because she believes that every person's breathing has a specific rhythm, which she needs to understand by physically observing one's breath and then teaching them diaphragmatic breathing. However, post-pandemic, she has started a retreat in Dapoli, Maharashtra, where people can go and stay for days to learn this life-transforming process. It's not mere healing—it's a way of life!

Well, this was about chanting. Apart from that, I also incorporate a 10-minute breathing practice in my morning routine. I just sit with my eyes closed and focus—like really focus—on each and every breath. It's a beautiful way of centering yourself. Maybe on a day-to-day level, these practices seem insignificant, but after three long years of practicing these tools daily, I feel their benefits are more like a compounding effect. One may take years to notice what change these smaller habits can make in your life. What made my TB journey (and the emotional wreck that it brought with it) *sufferable* was having a daily meditation routine.

TOOL 4: CONSUMING HEALTHY CONTENT

To feel better, I had to be mindful about what I consumed, not just the food but also the content. I started listening to podcasts that talked about health, behavioral change, neuroscience, and habit formation. I was (and still am) pretty serious about curating my healing and transforming my life. Given below is a list of my favorite speakers, whose podcasts kept me going and pulled me back - every single day from giving up on myself!

- Mel Robbins
- Jay Shetty
- Dr. Joe Dispenza
- Andrew Huberman
- Maya Shankar

All of this was about the tools that helped me untangle the 'mental' knots. While carefully trying to indulge in mindfulness, I realized that my 'physical' health and my workout had taken a back seat. Especially after May 2022, I used to feel that even waking up was a task. Not that I was not working out, but I was not consistent. I used to exercise for a day and then be a couch potato for three days in a row. The routine was quite erratic, and therefore I decided to gain some control over my physical health too.

TOOL 5: SETTING FITNESS GOALS

Somewhere in November 2022, my sister and I were watching a video on YouTube. It was about the right way of doing Surya Namaskar, the benefits of doing it regularly, and so on. Once we were done watching it, at 10.30 in the night, my sister looked at me and said, "How about doing 108 Surya Namaskar on January 1st, 2023? We still have like eight weeks to get there. Will you be able to do it?" With something like this thrown at me, I was confused at first, but then I realized I desperately needed some goal-setting—

something that I could look forward to and chase. I said yes, and then we began planning our schedule for the upcoming eight weeks.

2022, for me, had begun on a very sickly note. I had seen the first light of 2022 from a hospital bed. I wanted to change the narrative in the upcoming year. 2023 had to be great, and acing 108 Surya Namaskar on the very first day of the year was going to be my way of doing it. I was all excited! For those who wish to see how we progressed every week, this is our schedule.

Week No.	Weekend	No. Of Namaskars
Week 1	November 12	24
Week 2	November 19	36
Week 3	November 26	48
Week 4	December 3	60
Week 5	December 10	72
Week 6	December 17	84
Week 7	December 24	96
Week 8	December 31	108
	January 1	108

Just as we planned, we were able to reach our target. I must say that it was quite a journey, but I was amazed to see how my body was coping. On 1st January 2023, after completing the 108th Surya Namaskar, I was all welled up. I felt good, I felt strong, and I felt enthusiastic. Those intense eight weeks helped me bring consistency and discipline to my fitness journey. I knew that after this, I would never skip my workout, and now I am at a point where I love throwing physical challenges at myself. I love how exercise makes me feel. Even if I miss out one single day, I get cranky. The dopamine hit is something I genuinely look forward to. I also love watching videos about how exercise can impact your brain and your mood, and the results that I am witnessing are mind-blowing. One thing I know for sure is that I am never falling back into the 'not exercising phase' ever again.

I am amazed to see how tiny habits over a period of time can be extremely rewarding.

TOOL 6: FOOD FOR THOUGHT

Reading has been another therapeutic tool. Rather than considering my TB phase as a waste of time, I started looking at it as a vegetative state and took steps to broaden my horizons. I was anyway a voracious reader, but these years gave me more time to explore different genres and personalities. I profoundly invested my time in reading great plays, autobiographies, self-help books, and fiction. Some of the best people whose journey inspired me were Oprah Winfrey, Matthew McConaughey, Michelle Obama, Priyanka Chopra Jonas, Jay Shetty, and Anita Moorjani; their highs and lows truly served as a beacon of hope. I also revisited some of my old books and was amazed to see how differently we perceive the same pages at different stages of life.

I cannot even reckon the exact number of books that I read during my treatment. I am and will always be in awe of the power that knowledge carries. No matter how much you absorb, there is always room for something more!

On days when reading became saturating, I turned to watching movies. Since I had already started developing my own scripts for shorter formats, I started watching films with a screenwriter's eye. I also took online screenwriting lessons to have a better understanding of the structure.

Honestly, I never had any 'tangible' answers when people asked me what I was doing, but these years proved to be effective in fueling my creativity.

Apart from the ones that I mentioned above, here are a few more quick habits that I have incorporated in my routine:

- No cell phone before one hour of sleeping.
- No cell phone after one hour of waking up.
- Restricting the use of social media.
- Eat dinner by 7.30 p.m.
- Quit sugar and dairy.
- Maintain a gratitude journal.
- Keep going!!

This was a not-so-short summary of the little things that kept me going. Even after having such amazing tools at my disposal, I must say that I still do have bad days, and it's okay. I have realized that it's okay to not feel perfect at all times. But having said that, the bleak days shouldn't be an excuse for gliding into complacency. Your actions have the power to change how you feel, so no matter what happens, SHOW UP. Look in the mirror, raise your hand, and tell yourself that you are here. It shows your commitment to the kind of person you want to be. Don't feel like doing a full workout? Do it for five minutes. It reinforces your intention to become a person who doesn't miss workouts—this is what James Clear says in 'Atomic Habits'!

So, my tool kit helps me step back and look objectively at my bad days. It acts like my coping mechanism, ensuring that my fears and insecurities do not grow bigger. It helps me remind myself that what really matters is progress over perfection, and I am glad that with every passing day, I am getting closer to the 'I' that I am looking for!

#TakeYourPowerBack

CHAPTER 10

Spotting My Greenlights

My hospital check-ups have always been noteworthy, and I do not say it with an optimistic tone. Every time I went to the hospital, I used to find at least one patient who started their treatment on that very day. It was painful and sad. Right from the year I began my treatment, I have had strange encounters with the patients almost during every monthly follow-up. Later, I deliberately started striking a conversation with them just to understand their story, where they are coming from and what their world looked like. Maybe, subconsciously, I was doing it to minimize the intensity of my sorrow and pain. It made me look beyond myself and be grateful for what I had.

There were people who weren't responding to the treatment; some were the sole breadwinners of the house and hence were facing an economic crisis as they couldn't work. One of the patients was just unaware about where she was having an infection—whether she had EPTB or pulmonary TB. She was simply popping tablets months after months without knowing when it was going to end. People with poor educational backgrounds had no voice in the hospital simply because they couldn't ask proper questions.

The effects of their lack of education were seen on multiple fronts. And I do not mean bookish education, but general education about how one is supposed to stick to such a lengthy course of treatment, what precautions one has to take, how the tablets need to be taken, and so on. All of this needs to be properly communicated. I remember an incident when I was standing in a queue to get my medicines. A lady standing before me had come to collect her husband's medicines. As she went in, the newly appointed pharmacist asked her to show the previous month's remaining medicine packets. Generally, the packaging of the medicines keeps changing. The lady, just because she could not read, did not understand that she had the same tablet in two different types of packets and hence kept giving her husband the same medicine twice. Also, instead of giving half a tablet, as prescribed by the doctor, she kept giving him an entire tablet every day. The pharmacist realized what blunder had been happening—the poor patient was taking 1200 mg instead of 300 mg every single day for months! The previous pharmacist wasn't explaining anything to the patients. Later, the newly appointed fellow segregated all the tablets and, to avoid any confusion, marked the tablets with different colored markers. God bless him!

Another incident is where a girl, roughly my age, was being told, bluntly, that she had MDR and that she would need to quit her job right away and get hospitalized. After receiving so much information in just 20 seconds, the girl started crying. She started raising her concerns: she had piles, so she was worried if the tablets would worsen the situation, how would she cope with the heat the medicines generate in the body, and so on. She helplessly sat on the bench after receiving not-so-satisfactory answers. I got so mad at the hospital staff because I could see myself in her shoes. I had my throwback moment. I felt, how could the doctors reveal such sensitive information with zero consideration? Yes, I understand that it is an everyday thing for them, but it's a life-altering moment, not just for a patient, but also their entire family. At least in the hospital where I was taking my treatment, the doctors (and by that, I mean the interns who had just cleared their exams) always looked angry. They hardly used to look at the patients while talking. I understand keeping a certain physical distance; it's a part of safety, but why do they have to pick a rude tone every time? What kind of treatment is this? Never in my two years of treatment have I seen them talking to a patient with care and concern. Is that too much to ask for? I don't think so!

Every time I came back from the hospital, I used to narrate such painful incidents to my mother. I knew I had to contribute my bit towards the cause. I strongly feel that when a person is diagnosed with a deadly disease, they are not just supposed to 'go through' it but also 'take it forward' in some ways. I felt the responsibility. No matter how minuscule my role would be, I had to be in the picture. I needed a community—a **tribe**—that would have like-minded people. With this unexpressed rage in mind, I spoke to one of the top pulmonologists in the country. I decently vented out my agony and told him that I wish to do something about it. He calmly listened to everything that I had to say, smiled, and pulled a piece of paper. He wrote an email id and asked me to contact Mr. Chapal Mehra, a public health professional and founder of 'Survivors Against Tuberculosis' (SATB). I looked at the paper and sensed some hope! My first greenlight!

I immediately drafted an email and contacted SATB. Within a few days, I got their reply, saying that they would love to have a Zoom meeting with me. In the next couple of days, I officially became a TB advocate and SATB fellow. Through SATB, I have met some amazing people who once fought their rough battle against TB and are now inspiring others to not give up. SATB plays an important role in ensuring that there is enough survivor representation in the country's policy making. It is working day and night to provide better patient-centric care and is fighting incessantly for the patients' rights to receive better treatment. I have been a part of a couple of initiatives, and I intend to do more work in the coming years.

It was through my mentor there that one fine day I received an email from the US. It was regarding a research paper that one of the doctors from Harvard was conducting. My mentor thought I was the perfect candidate for the case study and, hence, recommended my name to the doctor there. The paper was questioning the effectiveness of shorter regimen and if it was really a better option. I had seen the painful side effects of the shorter regimen; my bone marrow was suppressed, and I had also fallen prey to neuropathy. With me as her case study, the doctor was getting to see everything in one patient. We kept communicating via email and Zoom. As I started writing more to her about my journey, she asked me if I would like to have my name as a co-author in the research paper! WAIT, WHAT? I took a while to process everything, and once I realized that it was happening for real, I immediately said yes. I still couldn't believe it, though. But yes, it was real, and I could finally believe my eyes when the paper got published in the PHA.

My first international collaboration! Pinch me, please!

Once I was done catching my second greenlight, I was pumped up to create some more of them for myself. I kept scratching my head thinking about what else could be done for the community, and that's when it struck me that World TB Day was around the corner!

For those who aren't aware, World TB Day is celebrated every year on 24th March. I had decided long ago that I would make a documentary and release it on TB Day. I was never really vocal on social media about me going through something like this. Nobody (apart from my close-knit circle) knew that I had TB. I had deliberately kept everything low-key. I was so scared of people asking me, "What are you doing these days?" that I had shut everything down. I wasn't on social media for a long time. I wanted to be brave enough to share my story, but I didn't want people to feel sorry for me. So, I thought about revealing it once I was close to finishing my treatment. I had completed my 21 months of treatment by March 2023. In three months, i.e., in June 2023, I was going to come off my medications. It felt like a perfect timing to shed my nervousness and come out of a shell. I started working on the documentary. I wanted it to be more holistic; my intention was not just to tell everyone what I have been through but to also educate people about TB. For this, I wanted my doctors to speak about TB and its types in a more colloquial manner. Naturally, I went to my doctors—this time the senior ones— and discussed with them the whole idea. I wanted to shoot their part in the hospital, for which they asked me to submit an application. In the days that followed later, I went to the hospital daily. Sadly, this is where my morale went down.

I was made to sit for hours and then being told to come the next day. To my horror, I was just asked to move from one department to the next with an application, which ultimately landed in the trash. Finally, after a week, I was being told to mind my own business. They disregarded my efforts by calling it a 'publicity stunt' and demeaned me in every possible way. My purpose behind doing all of this was never to highlight how insurmountable my journey was (I am fully aware that there are others who go through much more pain), but to point out the lesser-known facts about the disease and motivate those who are on the edge of giving up! It was heartbreaking to see such senior people make fun of their own patients. I cried on my way back home, feeling dejected. I thought it was a waste of time and energy. With shame creeping in, I almost decided to give up on the initiative. Just then I received a message from a senior lady doctor (who was present in the cabin when other senior doctors ridiculed me) 'indirectly' hinting that I should not feel bad because of some condescending misogynists (this happened on Women's Day, by the way, just saying because the irony was hard hitting!). She sent me a long text, telling me not to give up and that she would ask her friend from the private sector to help me with the bytes. The pulmonologist from the private sector agreed! So, on one hand, I was feeling despondent for not being taken seriously by my own doctors. But on the other hand, some other doctor, who was not even treating me, sounded more than excited to take me under her wings. One door closes, another door opens!

I am narrating the backstory because what happened behind the scenes is more important than the documentary itself. You will see ahead!

So, I picked a date for the shoot. 14th March, 2023. The shooting part—both mine and the doctor's—went very smoothly. I just had 10 more days to finalize everything. I was lucky enough to have friends coming over to help me in every department. The edit happened, the dubbing went well, and I thought, finally, it's happening! I sighed with relief.

On the 24th morning, I was all set to put a little teaser on Instagram. While discussing the 'hows' and 'whens' of the same, I was traveling by metro for work. As I got down from the metro, I realized I did not have my phone. I panicked because EVERYTHING - right from the video to the caption and the contact details of people who had worked on the documentary, was saved on my mobile phone. MY PHONE WAS STOLEN! Bam!!

I thought okay, with so many hurdles kicking in right from the beginning, maybe it's a sign that I shouldn't post the video. Once again, I was at the pinnacle of anxiety. My brain was frozen, and I felt there was no way to recover the data. The exchange of data was happening through WhatsApp. I was receiving all the links there because, for work reasons, I was staying away from my house for a week. I did not have my laptop. I was completely dependent on my cell phone, which I no longer had! Luckily, I was accompanied by a friend that day, so we kept calling on my number. The person who must have stolen the phone kept disconnecting our calls. I called my parents (I know their numbers by heart, thank God!) and told them everything—naturally, I was scolded for my recklessness—and they were 100 percent sure that I must have kept my phone on the metro seat and given an open invitation to the thief—come, steal it! In my defense, I do not remember keeping my phone on the seat! Anyway, moving on.

I have a family friend who used to be a metro pilot. My parents got in touch with him, and he pulled some strings. He made a few calls and let the metro staff know about the incident. All of this was happening back home, in Navi Mumbai. I was on the other end of the town, having no clue about how to navigate the situation. Meanwhile, the friend who had accompanied me kept calling on my number. I don't know how, but an hour later, somebody answered my number and told us that my phone was found at Ghatkopar metro station. I immediately told my parents, who then told my former metro pilot friend, who then told the staff at Ghatkopar metro to collect my phone and keep it safely with them. Since I was stuck at work, I could only leave for Ghatkopar in the evening. After providing my identity proof (along with some lashing), I got my phone back. It was around 6 p.m. Obviously, the idea of putting a teaser had gone down the drain. I quickly posted a story on Instagram saying that I would be dropping a video at 7 p.m., so stay tuned!

You are following me, right?

Around 6.55 p.m., I sat down with my phone to upload the video. I was still a little hesitant to post it. We live in a world where trolling or mocking has become a norm. I began thinking, what if someone comes up and tells me to shut up? I started having second thoughts. But I had to brush aside my doubts and go for it anyway!

I had come back on Instagram after several months. The hiatus from social media had one major drawback: I didn't know that IGTV wasn't a thing anymore. I couldn't post a five-minute video—not even as a reel. I asked my techno-savvy friends, but we couldn't find any solution. Meanwhile, my DMs were full with questions like, "It's already 7.30 p.m.; where is the video! There were some sarcastic messages too, but I preferred turning a blind eye towards them because I didn't want to escalate my anxiety. Even after relentless efforts, I failed to upload it on Instagram. Okay, now what?

In such clock-ticking situations, our mind tends to leave our body. But I had to come up with an alternative. After taking a couple of long breaths, I decided to open my YouTube channel and release the video on YouTube. But what about the long caption that I had written? So, I thought, let's post a recent picture (to reveal my current face) with the same long caption on Instagram and then put the YouTube link of the video in my bio. Sounds reasonable? Sorted! Let's do it!

It was 8.30 p.m. I was constantly on a call with my friends, who were helping me out. I created a channel and started the upload. But the house where I was staying that night did not have wi-fi, and since the video was heavy, my mobile data got exhausted right in the middle of the upload! Bam!!! I panicked! WHAT IS HAPPENING???? Too much drama in one single day, right? My friend sensed over a call that I was on the threshold of a nervous breakdown, and he quickly recharged my data pack. I did not have a proper network, so my internet connection was quite poor; hence, the upload took more than an hour. Finally, at 9.30 p.m., I finished uploading the video on YouTube, and everything was out—even on Instagram—by 9.45 p.m. BIG SIGH AND SCREAM!!!

I sank into a chair and kept my phone aside. I was flushed! I realized that I hadn't eaten anything at all, so I went to the kitchen to grab a bite. But guess what? My phone had almost started to explode with messages, calls, and cries! Honestly, I was anticipating a decent response, but I had absolutely not expected the flooding reactions—it was a major shocker! My colleague called me in the middle of his shoot after watching the video and was unable to speak because of the tears. A friend's friend rang my number and was at a loss for words. Even my distant relatives who had mocked me (unknowingly, of course) for my color change got to know the real reason behind it, and they were pouring love and care. I received calls and messages (really long ones) from the people who briefly knew me, and the sense of camaraderie was just gratifying. They really wanted to know if I was fine. It was the first time in all these months I felt that yes, I matter. People were sliding into my DMs, saying that their mother, their sister, or their house help was going through the exact same thing and that they would like me to talk to them once. In a virtual world where everything is superficial and transient, I discerned that authenticity wasn't exactly extinct; what I received was pure and genuine; I could sense it through my screen! That was my biggest aha moment, not because I was validated, but because I owned my story and hence felt liberated! More than the praise and love, what really touched me were the words of fellow MDR patients. They sounded positive and absolutely ready to fight the devil—my purpose was served. The critique in me was silenced. Immediately, I recalled Mark Twain's famous quote, "You are never wrong to do the right thing."

Once the buzz started fading, I took a moment to sit with everything. Before moving forward, I had to look inward. A few months before that day, I was questioning my worth, letting the outer situation strip away my confidence. But that night, I knew I was trying to re-anchor my foundation and solidify my sense of self. I was able to step away from the puddle and look myself in the eye. And I must say, I looked much, much better!

Should I let one disease define me? No… I need not keep fixating on one closed door and ignore the other 99 doors that opened for me. So many of my friends who were not in touch or had grown apart felt the need to rekindle the bond after watching the video, and I was absolutely onboard to give such friendships another chance! Why Not?

So yes, to the ones who are back... and to the ones who turned back... You humbled me!

And as Mel Robbins rightly says, every setback is preparing you for a set-up! To those who are battling tough situations and are wondering WHY ME, pick yourself and gear up, for a lot better is coming our way!!

Cheers!

#Aha

CHAPTER 11

Comfortable in My Skin

So much of our identity is linked to our external appearance. Isn't it? The way I look had changed over the course of two years. But yeah, for me, no regrets! One of the drugs, Clofazimine, has a very external, hence an obvious side effect: skin discoloration. The skin keeps getting darker as you keep taking the dose. It's a gradual change. To be honest, I never realized that my skin color was changing. Roughly two–three months after taking the treatment, one of my doctors pointed out that my skin tone seemed darker and that I used to look very fair before starting the medicines. Really? Okay!

During the initial months, nobody really observed it. But as months passed, I started looking reddish. After almost a year, the change became quite evident. I started having patches around my lips and my forehead. Also, after a year, I had started socializing a bit, so I was meeting people more often. They could immediately notice something 'different' and therefore used to bombard me with their comments. Some were mean. Some were funny. My father used to feel really bad about it. I was quite chilled out because color change was something so external that it didn't really bother me. Plus, I didn't have to look at myself as often as other people, so I was quite okay!

Since my father kept insisting that I seek a dermatologist's opinion and see if there was something to stop excessive tanning, I went to a dermatologist's clinic, quite against my will. I told him everything, especially my father's concerns regarding *"Log kya kahenge"* (not that my father attaches unnecessary importance to other people's views; he just didn't want to hear any hurtful words about me—again, thinking that the mean words might affect me mentally). I also told the doctor that I would not take any extra pills because that, just like me, would not be 'fair'! The doctor explained everything to us. He said that these medicines keep saturating their deposits under the skin. So, the tanning wasn't superficial; it was deeply seated in all the layers of my skin. It was really a good call that I didn't want to take anything extra to reverse it because the injections used for the same could interfere with the functioning of my heart (which, mind you, was already broken; just kidding). He also assured that the color change was reversible, meaning - once I stop the treatment, I would slowly, within a year or two, retain my original skin tone. Fabulous, right? I didn't see any problem there.

But somewhere in December 2022, i.e., one and a half years after taking the medicines, I started observing small spots on my neck—not a very fancy image! Within a month, I saw those spots spreading across my body. My dermatologist said that it was due to the extreme toxicity of the drug. There was no scope for more tanning, so the toxins were being thrown out in this form. These spots, he said, are not very common and therefore will not be reversible. They would lighten over a period of time, but they wouldn't go away completely.

My father panicked!

Since my elder sister's wedding was due in a month, we were expecting a lot of guests. A lot of guests would mean a lot of questions, for which we had to be prepared! Here is a list of some confused and cruel comments which I heard during those two years:

"Why do you look like a baked cake?"

"Do something about your color…it's looking bad."

"Can you make her look fair on the wedding day?"

"Try eating my handmade ladoos… Maybe they will make you look fair!"

"Hey, why have you put on makeup like an XYZ actress?" (who, by the way, has a dark complexion)

"Try this cream. It will work."

"Oh, so you have a guest at home?" someone to my parents. "What! Is this Akshata? I didn't recognize her"

"Why are you not taking any medicines for this 'problem'?"

"Damn, you used to look beautiful before!"

…and many more!! But my response was always very delightful. I don't think I would have been able to keep my cool had I not faced any internal complications. Color change and even other people's reactions to that seemed trivial. Also, I never complained because half of those people didn't know that I was taking medicines for MDR, so no grievances. Having said that, I am still addressing the comments that

I heard because it made me think about how society (still) equates 'beauty' with 'fairness'. Why does beauty need to have any color? I mean, yes, even I used to find it difficult sometimes to associate with my pictures because I was genuinely looking different, but I never considered myself 'not beautiful'.

Discoloration could bother a lot of patients because our core physical trait gets altered. You look in the mirror and feel like you are not looking at yourself; it could be a bit daunting. I never found that change *that* traumatizing because I had seen my mom go bald. She never had a dull moment, so there was no chance that I could have cribbed about me getting darker!

However, the only thing that hadn't changed was the color of my eyes—a solid hazel color! Some of my buddies told me that they could spot me in a crowd only because of the hazel-y eyes! Yea, my darling friends made me feel good by saying that my eyes looked even more defined because of my new complexion. Such sweethearts, aren't they?

They knew about my treatment and had seen my gradual discoloration. They did tell me that I was carrying myself really well. I was not putting any makeup on while going out because it never really served the purpose. There was no point in investing in the products, which, after a few years, would become useless. Even during my sister's wedding, I chose a person for the makeup who knew that makeup is not about 'becoming fair'. She beautifully retained my existing skin tone without putting layers of concealer. She was fab!

Honestly, I always loved a dusky complexion because I thought it was more earthy. Now that I had it, I was really enjoying trying different looks—long hair, short hair, no lip tint, smokey eyes, nose pins, and many more experiments which I never thought of doing before! Plus, I was on an acting sabbatical, so even if the experiments failed, I had nothing to lose. Win-Win!

With such solid backing, I wasn't allowed to feel bad. I enjoyed—quite literally—being in my own skin. I was trying new colors that would suit my tone. Also, with regular workouts, I was feeling good about my body too. It was time for some change—some serious flaunting! So yes, a short skirt, a dusky complexion, a bold red lipstick (sometimes), open, messy hair, and an unwavering self-confidence— self-confidence, yes, what else does beauty stand for?

With a kickass attitude and without any heels, I had crushed 23 months of treatment under my neuropathic feet. Now it was time for a new chapter. Some good news, some celebration, some endings, and some beginnings!

#Finally

CHAPTER 12

Finishing Strong

Oh my God!! We are here, aren't we? In May 2023, I entered the 23rd month of my TB treatment. This month is anyway one of my favorites because I celebrate my birthday on May 5th. Though the month had begun on a dim note, I managed to treat myself well on my birthday by watching a smashing run of 'Sound of Music' followed by enjoying a solo dinner at Social's. Also, I slowly resumed my work. I had started rehearsing for a play after a freaking gap of three years. Things were falling in place! I was told that my treatment would end in June, so I was sincerely following my routine.

On May 22nd, I paid a visit to the hospital to ask my doctors if any tests were required before coming in June to stop the treatment. My doctor looked at me and said that there was no need to wait till June first week. "Come back on the 24th with a few test reports, and I will stop your treatment," she said. I was still not ready to believe those words because I was told many times in the past that my treatment would be stopped, but nothing ever happened. Earlier, it was supposed to stop in November 2022, which then became December 2022. In December, they said we will see what happens in January 2023. In January, they were like, "No, sorry, let's wait till March," and in March, I was told to continue the treatment till June and complete a 24-month course. It was a matter of pushing myself for two more weeks, so I never really expected the good news to come any sooner.

I came home and told my parents about the same. We got the tests done, and on the 24th morning, I went to the hospital by myself. I was very casual and did not carry any hopes. In my head, I was prepared for yet another disappointment. The hospital was relatively less crowded that day. I could not see many patients around, so I was called in for a checkup pretty quickly. The doctor looked at all my reports, right from June 2021, and glanced at my file for 10 good minutes. I am not sure I was ready to hear what she was going to say. Just then a stream of words came from her mouth: "Congratulations; you are no more a TB patient now." She signed the file and put her stamp to close my case.

WHAT??????

The words lashed on my ears like a wave. My heart skipped a beat, and I couldn't believe my ears and eyes. I tried wrapping my head around reality. The moment that I was desperately waiting for was finally there after one year, eleven months, and fifteen days! My knees felt weak, and my throat was lumpy. I came out of the cabin and sat in the lobby. For a while, I felt stuck—stuck between the years that had gone by and the days that lay ahead. Sometimes we wait for something so desperately that when we finally have it, we find it cold, strange, and almost unfamiliar. In my head, I had imagined this day so many times that when it was actually happening, I didn't know what to do with it. I took a good look around the lobby, a place that stood as a testimony to so many life-altering events. I went back to my very first day at the hospital, when, like a fool, I had directly asked for my tablets, having zero idea that my life was at the precipice of change. I had quick flashes of everything—literally everything—how I had walked in the first time wearing a blue t-shirt and black jeans, how my parents had brought me there a month later after my knees were locked, how I was trying not to throw up every time I went for a checkup, how I was forced to eat before swallowing a tablet, how painful it was to get pricked by a needle every week, how I was losing my hair in bunches, how my parents were pushing my wheelchair, how I was told that everything will be okay, how I was managing to stay put... And finally today... how lonely I felt...with no one around to share such a massive piece of information.

I recalled what my late aunt used to say during her last days: "If your one hand aches, your other hand cannot carry that pain on its behalf. The hurting hand has to endure the suffering on its own." Though I had my family members standing strong by my side, in these two years, whatever emotional and physical pain I went through, I only had to bear it myself. Yes, family support meant a lot, but the pain is and should be only yours to endure. That is what resilience is, isn't it? I saw myself in different phases with different faces—sometimes happy and sometimes sad. I had finally cleared my eclipse!

With a big sigh, a tear trickled down my eyes. I was feeling so many things at once that shedding a tear was the only relevant outcome. You cry when you are sad, you cry when you are happy, and you cry when you don't know what to feel. I shut my file and kept it in my bag. I took out my box of tablets and was ready to pop it in one last time. But before that, I took a close look at it. I stared at the tablet really hard and expressed my gratitude. Though they had given me a hard time, had I not taken them religiously, I would not have seen this day. I was finally TB-negative. Yes!!

I was so immersed in processing the moment that I had forgotten to ring my parents and share the news with them. Their first reaction that I heard over a call was just priceless. I could only imagine how happy and relieved they must have been. In those three years since the pandemic... I saw my mother go through her cancer phase, and later I myself fought a life-threatening disease. I was both - an observer and a bearer. And I must say that watching a person suffer is more painful than the actual suffering. I know my parents were more worried; they must have had more sleepless nights than I did. But not even once did they ever frown and create a sense of fear. They were always optimistic, supportive, caring, and loving. At times when I inadvertently took out my frustration on them, they were calm and composed. Although I was 'a patient', I needed to learn what it means to 'be patient'. I can never, ever thank my stars enough for blessing me with such a solid support system. I know I have never said any of these things out loud. I get awkward while expressing affection. So, this book is my attempt to express a deep sense of love and respect to my parents and my dearest sister and tell them that I am nothing without you three! I love you! (Okay...BRB)

So, coming back, I hung up their call, took my belongings, and was set to step my foot outside. I stood at the main gate of the hospital and turned around. It just dawned on me that there could be someone who is walking inside through the gates and starting their treatment today. Suddenly, everything seemed transient. But I was not going to let that feeling take away my sense of liberation. Keeping those patients in mind, I stepped outside the hospital. I had successfully crossed over to the other side—the one with no medicines, no pain, and no suffering! And now it was my duty—as a MDR-TB 'survivor'—to empower other patients to successfully carry out this long yet worthwhile transition.

I had definitely finished strong, and now I was entering a new chapter of my life, a chapter that needed me to be more strong, more healthy, more disciplined, and more resilient. But more than that, I had to be prepared with an answer to a question that always managed to scare the hell out of me: What's next?

#OntoTheNextPhase

CHAPTER 13

What's Next?

I really wish I had fancy, clap-worthy answers to this question, but sadly, I don't have any!

After coming home and sharing the news with my parents, we had a small celebration at my sister's place—yes, she's a married woman now. My father just wanted to throw away all the remaining tablets and discard the box forever (which we did a few days later, and I must say we had a whole ceremony for that). Everyone bestowed their blessings and wished me luck. I had a big finish, and now I was at the threshold of a new life that was waiting for me. I genuinely did not have anything planned. The only thing I knew was to stay healthy, take each day as it came, and just keep moving. A sense of direction would have been nice, but I took a deep breath and centered myself. I was with my people, but I strongly knew that once I was alone, I would burst into tears. Post-lunch, I went inside a room and locked myself for a while. I wasn't really feeling ecstatic, and I was wondering why. I didn't want to, but I kept going back. It was on this exact same day last year that things in my personal life had taken a sharp turn. A YEAR HAD PASSED. REALLY? I welled up thinking about how shattered I was back then. I had mixed feelings about everything, in general. I cried for two good hours, penned down my feelings, and then felt much better. I told myself that had all of this not happened, I would not have stood up for myself. Wiping your own tears makes you tough, and I sure as hell am a tough nut to crack. I knew I had to leave those tears behind and gear myself up for everything good that lay ahead. Brushing away all the heaviness, I sprang out of bed and got ready to leave for my rehearsals.

Well, they say you can't move forward if you keep looking back. But I feel that sometimes you need to look back and see how far you have come. I always thought that those three years—which include one year of pandemic and two years of treatment—gave me a major setback in life. But now I think "it wasn't really a deviation from the path... it WAS the path" (I really wish I could remember who said this line).

TB just came into my life out of nowhere. But it ended up giving me some tough yet valuable life lessons. Today, when I look in the mirror, I cannot really see my older self—not just because of the discoloration, but because I think I have truly transformed into a different human being. Sometimes it is hard to accept everything, but it was this journey that brought me closer to my real self and made me understand what my non-negotiables are. My strength, my patience, my faith, and my love (for myself) were being put to test…and I would like to believe that I graciously passed with a solid 'A'!

In my professional life, I do have a few things in mind, which I am sure would unveil as the time goes. One thing I can share is that acting has and will always be my first love. It's not going anywhere, but what kept me sane every single day was writing, a newly discovered tool that I am never letting go of. I sometimes wonder if I can juggle between two career options, but every time my self-doubt kicks in, I manage to keep my head above the water and bring myself back to the present moment.

To sound more pragmatic, I am sharing a small instance. When I was in the middle of writing this book, I had occasional moments where self-doubt was creeping in. Everything just boiled down to one single question: "Does my story matter?" The answer in my head was not a very pleasant one. I used to feel worthless, and for three good months, I had stopped writing. I felt it was a big fiasco because how can I be a professional writer if I can't put down five words on a page? Wasn't this book supposed to be my first step towards embracing a new parallel profession?

Am I a failure? Am I not good enough for this? Am I good at anything at all? Maybe not!!! Let's just give up!!

I think I almost had! One evening, after my leg was severely hurt, I was feeling 'blahhh'. Since I couldn't work out properly, I was doing some stretching. In my head, I was not saying 'wow' things about myself. And just then, I got a random call from a friend. We hadn't spoken in years. He just said, "I look up to you…You are so brave. Keep going, girl," and he hung up! I kept wondering what just happened. I don't know if I should call this a divine intervention or synchronicity, whatever you name it. I feel it was the universe's way of guiding me and telling me to shut up and just do the work! I resumed writing!

Unplanned and, of course, unwanted changes throw you off for a while. And in cases of diseases like MDR-TB, where the treatment is not just toxic but also painfully long, it is very

obvious that your mental health deteriorates. At such times, you feel like you have to scream and vent your anger, but at the same, you feel that no one can understand you. And that is why you want someone to just - no solution, no advice… no breakthrough— just simply listen! And that is why I have been earnestly listening to all the patients who slide into my DMs. I never expected people to approach me like this, but the documentary posted on TB Day did some wonders. A lot of people watched it, and since then have been keeping in touch with me. Even they know that I am not a doctor who can magically cure them, they just need an empathetic ear... someone who has been through what they are battling—to tell them that it's going to be okay.

Let no one, not even your own voice, tell you that you can't do it. It is going to be tough, but we are going to be even tougher! So, to everyone out there, especially DR-TB patients who are feeling rage for missing out on opportunities, for having setbacks in career, for having broken family ties, for not knowing what's next... I believe that you are strong. We all are…we just need to change the story we tell ourselves. It's going to be freaking hard, but it's all going to be worth it. Everything is going to make sense, and I am waiting for that day! I believe it's coming very soon—not just for me but for all of us. But till then, hold on. Stay put, and don't you ever dare give up on yourself.

Sharing my journey has been cathartic and liberating. I have raised my authentic voice, and I am willing to hear yours. Every time you feel dissuaded, every time low self-esteem knocks in... Every time you ask yourself if your story matters, let your inner voice tell you that it's a yes—a big yes—your story matters! And if you don't tell your story, someone else will!

I intend to create a space where more stories are told and more voices are heard. We cannot end the taboo by having hush-hush around the topic. Let's not fear, but hear each other. There is a great power in showing your courage. A lot has been done before, and yet a lot more needs to be done. I believe in spreading the light; I believe in lifting each other up; I believe that it all works out for good, and I am going to keep believing. For me, this is how we heal!

To all those who are feeling eclipsed, to all those who are healing while dealing with that feeling, this was my story, and this is what I proudly own!

#HealingWhileDealingWithTheFeeling

A Day Before I Submitted the Manuscript: An Excerpt From My Diary

9th November, 2023

Today, exactly a year ago (9th November 2022), I had started writing the book. Never thought I would come this far. It feels like a full circle. Writing this book has truly been therapeutic for me. It's been six months since I have finished my treatment. Soon after I stopped taking the medicines, I learned about the acute shortage of drugs—patients all over the country were not getting medicines, and as of the given date, things are erratic. Not being able to take the medicines for months is putting the lives of the patients in danger. I know what happened to me when the doctors had stopped my drugs for just 20 days—the disease is lethal and brutal. Patients cannot *not* have the medicines; they can't afford to take gaps in the course. The issue is serious and needs some attention from the concerned authorities. WE CANNOT HAVE MEDICINES GO OUT OF STOCK!

On the professional front, things are almost taking off (fingers crossed). I am about to submit the manuscript for this book. Hahh! There is a long way to go. I am looking forward to doing many more things and making my parents super proud. And you never know; maybe next time this year, I could be working on my second book. Anything can happen, but now in a good way!

To all good things!

Cheers! See you on your bookshelves!

Acknowledgment

I cannot wait to mention all those names and all those people who have encouraged me to pursue this treacherous yet satisfying endeavor.

Firstly, my mom and dad—they are one solid team. They were there—literally there. I know they will always be. I love you.

My sister, who is my all-time cheerleader, I can never thank you enough.

Vinit Tamhankar, my brother-in-law, who came up with the title and shot the lovely cover image. You were more enthusiastic than I ever was. You saved me!

Prakash Dashputre, Ameya Mondkar—you folks went through my piece when it was blooming and budding.

Apoorva Bhatt, for being my first critic. You chose to step in as my proofreader when I had nothing. Thank you for all that ear-pinching. Your dedication and literary suggestions pushed me to complete the book in time. Big love!

Natasha Jacob for vigilantly reading each and every page. You are such a sweetheart!

Aakanksha Monga, Geet Hazarika, Alok Vaidya, Jovy Philip, Dr. Gita Mohan, Rutvij Dashputre, Yogita Deshmukh, and Jaydeep Nerlekar—for helping me figure out how to land a publisher, for guiding me with the legal contracts, and for periodically keeping a track of my progress!

Chapal Mehra, SATB I guess I will always have you by my side!

Notion Press and the entire team for being the wind beneath my wings. You made it happen. Biggest thanks! Fiction Foxx for designing the cover page, you have always been my greenlight!

Last but not the least – all my friends and extended family members who were silent supporters in this amazing journey I have had so far. I know you will always have my back through thick and thin. Pure love!

Can I be more grateful?

Notes/Reference

Chapter 5: Why so foul?

Articles on parosmia:

https://www.healthline.com/health/parosmia-after-covid#duration

https://www.nytimes.com/2021/06/15/health/covid-smells-food.html

https://www.thecut.com/2021/09/covid-19-parosmia-sense-smell.html

ASHA Workers

https://indianexpress.com/article/explained/explained-who-asha-workers-women-healthcare-volunteers-who-7932479/

Chapter 6: Ouch my feet

It was getting me ready to walk the road less traveled, because that was going to make all the difference! Robert Frost: The road not taken

Chapter 7: Living with neuropathy

Exercises for neuropathy

https://www.youtube.com/watch?v=loUuq7rPTH0&t=227s

Chapter 8: Bitter ending or better beginning?

Healing is never linear - Jennifer Lawrence on 'Actors on Actors' with Viola Davis.